HOW FREE
DO YOU WANT
TO BE?

All my Best

HOW FREE DO YOU WANT TO BE?

STEPS TO A SPIRITUAL AWAKENING

—

THE STORY OF A CURE FOR ADDICTION

R. CORD BEATTY

DEDICATION

I want to dedicate this book to my Creator. Your love and way of life are everything to me. Thank you from the bottom of my heart for picking me up when I stumbled and fell. Everything I am and have, I owe to you, your love, and your way of life. I am grateful for the words you have given me in writing this book. They were divinely inspired and freely given.

To my children and family. My journey back was a long and challenging road. Your unconditional love was the strength I needed to see me through. Thank you for not giving up on me. I am grateful that you are in my life and love each one of you dearly.

To the memory of every person who has fallen into the clutches of addiction, mental health issues and is no longer with us. To those of you who are still suffering. Your journey has some of life's most significant challenges ahead. You can overcome them with courage, the help of a loving God, and the support of others who have been where you are. My prayer is that this book helps you find the answers you have been seeking.

God's plan for each one of us is perfect in every way, predetermined, and set forth for us long before we ever came to this world. We need to remember to ask him where we are supposed to go.

To those of you who are still struggling, if you are reading this message, please hear me. You do not need to suffer the way that you have been for so long. You are not alone . . .

–R. Cord Beatty

CONTENTS

PROLOGUE

I opened my eyes to find myself staring at a beautiful bluebird on the window sill outside my room. The bird just stared right back at me for the longest time. For a minute, I thought I was dead. There was no pain in my abdomen or my throat. I felt peace and calm. The night before had been a painful hell, but this morning all the anger, depression, fear, and anxiety had gone. I wondered: *Has my prayer been answered?*

The nurse came in and asked if I wanted my pain meds for the morning. I said, "No, I don't think I need it right now."

I watched TV in silence all day long and didn't make any phone calls. I ate some food for the first time in a long time and didn't feel like doing much, talking, or anything at all. I waited all day for the pain to come back . . . It didn't.

The next morning, I opened my eyes, and my bluebird was back. Just staring at me through the window. The bird stayed for quite some time, and I wondered if it was real or I was delusional. No pain. No anxiety. No fear. No depression. I felt at peace. So much peace, it was puzzling. I wondered: *Is this the spiritual awakening I've been searching for? Is this the defining moment others have described?*

My doctor came to visit and asked how I was feeling? I told him I wasn't experiencing any pain. He looked puzzled, took out his light out, and pointed it into my eyes. Then he stepped back and said, "Mr. Beatty? You have something going on here. I want to order another biopsy." I refused and told him I was going home. He said, "You most certainly aren't!" I insisted I would be leaving soon one way or another—with his permission or not.

He said, "Fine, you'll be leaving against medical advice."

I told him, "I figured so."

I was acutely aware that my condition was critical, and physical recovery, survival, was a long way ahead, but, as I left the hospital, I felt God's presence all around me. I was at peace and felt serenity like I had never experienced before. It was as if angels were surrounding me, keeping me safe, watching over me. I knew that, in this instance, God was doing for me what I couldn't do for myself. I had just experienced the power of God for the first time in my life, and it was the beginning of my life of freedom and sobriety.

HOW FREE
DO YOU
WANT
TO BE?

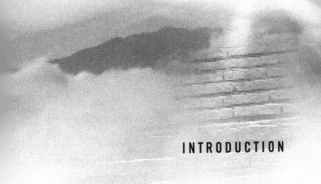

NEW PATH
TO FREEDOM

Everyone on this Earth experiences hardships. Everyone's burdens are different. What is a "life crisis" for one person, another might call "nothing at all," and others experience more trauma, anxiety, depression, or health issues in their lives than you or I could ever imagine? We all have our cross to bear as they say. What separates us is the weight and size of it and how far uphill we have to haul it. These crosses often involve mental health problems due to or arising from an addiction of one type or another—but these issues can be healed, and the truth is, as I've told many people I've worked with over the years, "We're all crazy? we just need to learn to hide it a little better, that's all." And the truth is we are all addicted to something. It might not be alcohol or drugs. It could be sex, gambling, pornography, playing video games, working, exercising, eating, shopping, hoarding, cleaning, even pain? The list goes on Infinitum.

Mental health issues were recorded as far back as 1900 BC, but around 400 BC, a Greek physician named Hippocrates identified the different levels of mental and physical health and, for the first time in history, endeavored to separate religion and superstition from health and well-being. He believed that bodily fluids—including, blood, bile, and phlegm, and lack of or excess thereof—were responsible for all mental and physical illnesses. He also believed mental illness was something to be ashamed of and must be punished. Thankfully a lot has changed since then.

Alcoholism and addiction were recorded as far back as 7000 BC. Since fermented beverages were developed in China and the existence of any mind-altering substances, in fact. In our society, alcohol, and drugs have always been at the root of illegal activity, problems, and several mental health disorders. The Volstead Act or Prohibition Act was passed by the United States Congress in 1919, making the distillation, sale, distribution, and transportation of alcohol illegal—but not its consumption. For the next 13 years, Americans proved that even the law couldn't keep them from a drink. Not only would they continue to use alcohol, but they would also profit from it as well via the black market. So despite attempts by the authorities to control alcohol, the problem was out of control. As one establishment was raided and closed down, another would pop up in its place.

The illegal use of alcohol also came with gangsters, moonshiners, and organized crime, and to add to the growing problem, the Italian mafia started to distribute heroin and cocaine. Like alcohol, the ever-increasing issues associated with the illegal distribution of drugs eventually led to the national prohibition of cocaine with the passing of The Dangerous Drug Act in 1920. Before this, heroin was regulated by the Harrison Narcotics Tax Act in 1914. The act made the sale and distribution of heroin legal for medical purposes only with a doctor's prescription, but by 1924, new laws made heroin an illegal substance.

During prohibition, medical doctors even began to prescribe alcohol as a way around prohibition, and, at one time, it was estimated that more than a million gallons of alcohol were prescribed per year. When prohibition was repealed in 1933, approximately 15 to 20 million Americans suffered from alcoholism. It's also true there have always been people who can drink moderately, those who can take it or leave it, hard drinkers, and those who can't stop drinking no matter what. Medical professionals and scientists have never really been sure about the cause of alcoholism, or addiction for that matter, but have identified specific things that lead to it— family history, drinking for long periods, mental health, anxiety, depression, and social acceptance, to name a few. However, not everyone with these issues becomes an alcoholic.

In the past, alcoholism and addiction were perceived as character flaws or a conscious decision of someone with no morals, honesty, or control by "normal" society's standards, and so sufferers were stigmatized. Thankfully all of this has changed over the years and particularly since the medical profession came forward and publicly declared alcoholism and addiction as "diseases." Since then, treatment has evolved substantially.

TWO PIONEERS IN THE HISTORY OF ALCOHOL REHABILITATION

Alcohol rehabilitation started as early as 1750 when groups of Native Americans formed "sobriety circles" to help members of their community stay sober. More than 100 years later, a doctor named Leslie Keeley in 1879 labeled "drunkenness" a legitimate medical disease and claimed he could cure it with injections of "Bichloride of Gold" (gold and chlorine). Keeley's operations may have been the earliest makings of what we know as residential inpatient treatment centers today. He formed the Keeley Institute, which operated out of expensive luxury homes, creating spa-like surroundings. Patients were pampered while receiving four injections of Bichloride daily. From 1879 to 1965 Keely opened and operated over 200 branches in the United States and throughout Europe.

However, in the history of alcoholism, two individuals, Bill Wilson (Bill W.) and Dr. Robert Holbrook Smith (Dr. Bob) stand out, when they came together in 1935 to form what is now known as Alcoholics Anonymous (AA). They were passionate about the cause because they were both desperate to stop drinking. Shortly after Bill W. became sober, he helped Dr. Bob to stop drinking too. Soon afterward, Alcoholics Anonymous was formed. Their initial plan was to work with alcoholics at the Akron City Hospital in Ohio, and, at first, the only people in the group were Dr. Bob, Bill W., and a mutual friend named Ebby Thacher (Ebby T.). These early pioneers also began writing a guidebook about how to become and stay sober. In 1939, the first edition of *Alcoholics Anonymous* was published, and the world started to learn about the success and methods of the authors called the "12 Steps."

In 1956, the American Medical Association declared alcoholism an illness and a disease. Before this time, hospitalization and mental wards were the only answer, and "patients" were treated with large amounts of alcohol in an attempt to make them so sick that they wouldn't want to drink again. At that time, alcoholism as was described as "drunkenness," "a personal choice," or "an uncontrollable alcohol habit." Many doctors advertised cures, but there were no treatment or detox centers, just peddlers of elixirs, potions, liquid cocaine, and similar preparations.

Today, new treatment centers spring up every day all over the world, offering treatment for alcohol, drugs, and every form of addiction—including sex, eating disorders, pornography, and all mental health issues. Most treatment centers offer residential inpatient programs, as well as outpatient treatment and sober living services. Some of them also offer detoxification. Along with group therapy and the traditional 12 Step program, these centers also provide individual therapy, adventure therapy, wilderness programs, cognitive thinking modalities, high tech electro-encephalogram therapies, hypnotherapy, and various types of classes and activities. These advances in treatment mean alcoholism and addiction are widely accepted as diseases.

In the early days of Alcoholics Anonymous, very few people had read the book or been through the 12 Steps. The program was designed as a simple way to experience spiritual awakening and psychic change. The early AA groups typically shared the message of hope by taking another alcoholic through the 12 Steps in one to two days with four to five one-hour sessions. Most of the time, they would require that all newcomers completed the 12 Steps before introducing them to regular meetings. They wanted others to hear from their experiences, and follow the directions in their book because then "the promises found within the 12 Steps will free you from alcoholism." They believed by following and living the examples of their 12 Step spiritual program, the cravings and compulsion to drink alcohol or use drugs would be removed.

Alcoholics Anonymous was the first time I faced my own addictions and mental health issues. I remember attending my first meeting, and the first time I read the book. It was very confusing.

I was like a deer in the headlights—full of fear and overwhelmed because I had never been through anything like the 12 Steps before.

I've often have wondered what it might be like for people attending their first meeting of AA or Narcotics Anonymous (NA) if they had already completed the 12 Step program before attending? If prayer and meditation was already part of their daily life? If they had already experienced a spiritual awakening and physic change? If they had a genuine connection with a higher power or God? Their chances of success and recovery from addiction might be much higher, you would think?

During the 1940s, the success rate of the AA program was around 75 to 80 percent of all newcomers remained sober and free from alcoholism. Today, that number is much lower. Published studies show the success rate at somewhere between 5 and 10 percent and only between 2 and 3 percent in some states and areas. As we'll explore in more depth later in the book, I hope that this companion to the 12 Steps will help make them more approachable and bring you the outcome you need.

EXPERIENCING THE 12 STEPS

For the duration of this book, I will be referring to the same 12 Steps as they were written in what I call the "Big Book," aka *Alcoholics Anonymous*, that was designed to lead to a spiritual awakening and psychic change. I would prefer to call them "proposals," "suggestions," or experiences because the word "steps" sounds too much like a test that must be passed to find sobriety. However, for simplicity, I will use the word steps as it is simpler—but it's not about pass or fail. Instead, I encourage you to think of the 12 Steps as an experience we will have together. Just like a mentor did with me. Just as they did in the 1940s.

These 12 Steps are clearly just suggestions that can guide you to a spiritual awakening, which causes a psychic change. A change in the way you think. For that reason, I will be sharing a way through these steps that made more sense to me than anything I had done before. And a process that created a spiritual awakening and a psychic change in my thinking. This is the same process that restored my mental health and led me to sobriety many years ago, and I now use to help others to find freedom through sponsorship and my treatment center.

We will be talking about alcoholism and addiction in general. However, the principles can be applied to every drug addiction and mental health issue. They can also be used to overcome every problem in your life—eating disorders, smoking, sexual addictions, pornography, anxiety, depression, chronic pain, mental disorders, and even personal relationships. Every troubling issue in your life can be overcome through the promises found within these 12 Steps.

I say this with conviction because I'm not just a recovered alcoholic. I consider myself an addict in general, and someone who has suffered from various mental health issues. I was an everything, never enough kind of guy. For most of my adult life, I suffered from alcoholism, drug addiction, anxiety, chronic depression, and delusional disorders, so this process is for anyone suffering from any of these issues or more.

The spiritual principles of the 12 Steps as they were taught in the 1940s and 1950s worked for thousands of men and women who found sobriety from their teachings. It worked for me, and it will work for you. Why change something that works? Just like them, when a mentor took me through the 12 Steps, in the same manner, I was told that following the directions would allow me to realize the promises held within the steps, and I would be free from alcoholism, addiction, and mental health issues for good. This was the case for me.

Before this, I'd been through seven different treatment programs without success. Each one about the same. I was given assignments on the first three steps and then usually started work on Step 4 before finishing the program and going home. I would leave and always drink the day or night I returned home. Sometimes on my way home. Nothing changed, and nothing stopped me from drinking alcohol or using drugs—not even jail until an alcoholic/addict took me through the 12 simple suggestions just as it was taught by those in the 1940s. Doing the step work freed me from compulsions and cravings and, by sharing this same process with you, my experiences, and a message of hope, you will have the same experience that I did.

I don't wish this book to be interpreted as a study guide for *Alcoholics Anonymous* nor stand on my soapbox and tell you that there is only one way to do this. I do have a strong opinion the only path to sobriety is a spiritual one—whatever that means to you and whatever you name it—but I'm not here to cause an argument or debate. I'm simply here to tell you that if you approach these 12 Steps with an open heart and mind, you will have an experience you haven't yet had in your life. You will discover things about yourself that you probably didn't know. Moreover, you're likely to find how we approach the 12 Steps in this book is quite different and I've witnessed people with years of long-term sobriety being mentored by someone who has only been sober a few months because they had gone through the steps, in the same manner, we will be going through. I always found this confusing until I experienced it for myself.

It started when I was attending an AA meeting in my early sobriety, and a young man named Ben was sharing. He was talking about the young men that he had helped through the 12 Steps. What struck me most about Ben was that he was all of about 18 years old, and here he was offering to sponsor anyone who needed one. I approached this young man after the meeting and asked him if I could talk to him for a few minutes. I asked him how long he had been sober. He said five years. I said, "That doesn't make a lot of sense, you're only 18?"

He told me that he became addicted to heroin and alcohol at about 12 years old. That his parents used heroin and alcohol daily when he was very young, and he had been offered both from a very young age. They would tell him that it was okay for him to use alcohol and drugs as long as it was at home. He quickly became an alcoholic and then moved on to heroin. His parents didn't care that he was sick and addicted. When he was 12 years old, he ran away from home and taken in by a family that got him into an addiction treatment center. There he found a mentor that took him through the 12 Steps very quickly and has worked with him since. His mentor understood that Ben needed to have a spiritual experience and needed the promises that come from doing the program.

Ben described how he worked at a wilderness program for young men and sponsored anywhere between 5 and 10 men privately. He said most of them were younger than him but some older. I was shocked, and impressed, to say the least, and he is the most remarkable young men I've ever met.

SOBRIETY IS MORE THAN JUST NUMBERS

Here is what I know from my own experience. Years of sobriety are just numbers, nothing more. They don't make success. Proof of this can be found in every AA or NA meeting room. Here you'll witness individuals walking up to the front to take a newcomer chip for attending their first meeting or first 24 hours of not using. I can tell you something about this because I did it for an extended period before I fully recovered from my alcoholism and addiction. I would get a little sobriety and then relapse over and over, always taking a newcomer chip and starting over.

Receiving a one-year, two-year, five-year, or 10-year achievement coin or chip, isn't what got me sober, nor is it what keeps me sober today. What does is my daily connection with God, prayer, meditation, mentorship, and service for others still suffering. The simple concept of one alcoholic working with another alcoholic or addict and sharing the message of hope with someone who suffers keeps me close to God and my sobriety.

What I'd like to encourage you to do is to have an open mind as we walk through this journey together. If you follow what the pioneers of the process tell you to do, you will experience what they experienced in the early 1940s. *Alcoholics Anonymous*, as it was written and first published in 1939, is an excellent publication and gives the 12 Steps, however, it can be somewhat challenging to understand, and usually requires someone who has knowledge of the writings to help you.

To begin this process, I would like to suggest reading the foreword, "Doctor's Opinion," and then the next 164 pages to help you gain a basic understanding before we walk through the 12 Steps in the following chapters. A copy of *Alcoholics Anonymous* can be purchased at most book resellers or online. If you are new to the process, this book will assist you in understanding the 12 Steps as a path to a full recovery. It should be fun and easy for you to follow along. As we journey through this process, we will reference some of what is found in the writings and teachings of the 12 Steps.

Again, just to be clear. Please don't confuse this process with some kind of test that must be passed to have a spiritual experience or to find sobriety. These suggestions are simply a guide to allow you to have your own experience. I also want to say that you must understand:

You can't go through these steps too quickly.

You can, however, go through them too slowly. This is because these suggestions hold within them specific promises that lead to a spiritual awakening, which causes psychic change. Changes in the way you think.

Remember, if you are still suffering, you are still very sick. You need the power of that comes from these promises now. Not six months from now.

Many times, I've heard things like:

- "You're too early in sobriety to be doing anything except the 1st Step."
- "You shouldn't be working on your 4th and 5th Steps for 6 to 12 months."
- "You shouldn't sponsor anyone unless you have at least 12 months of continuous sobriety."
- "The 4th and 5th Steps are the hardest ones and will take you a very long time to get through them".
- "The only way to ever be sober is to get the Big Book, get a sponsor, attend an AA meeting once a day, and ask God to keep you sober just for today."

Are you kidding me?

There is no way I would be able to stay sober if I thought the only way was to attend a meeting every day of my life. If I had to call my sponsor every day to receive instructions on what or what not to do next. If I had to ask God to keep me sober just for today. What about asking God to keep me sober for life? I couldn't live this kind of existence. I'd be drinking before sundown trying to make it through a day like that!

In this book, I'd like to encourage you to follow the process as it was intended. To work the steps with someone who understands them as they were outlined? To have a spiritual experience of your own. To enjoy a connection with God or higher power that you've never had before and asked for a compulsion to use drugs and alcohol be removed for good. What's wrong with that?

This is the way they did in the 1940s, and it worked for them. It has worked for thousands and thousands of men and women before you and me. It worked for me many years ago. Why wouldn't it work for you today?

If you're reading this book, then you have come to a crossroads in your life where you haven't or can't find the answers you need, and you are searching. You are reading various books. You are seeking answers to the issues in your life. Sometimes in the wrong places. After all, happiness is not a person, place or thing. It is a state of mind. As I said, you may have already been through the 12 Steps or working through them and can't stay sober? Maybe like me, you are a chronic relapser? If you can relate to this, you need the promises found in the 12 Steps, and you need them NOW!

As I've already described, the pioneer of these fundamentals, Bill W., was only a few days sober when he shared the message of hope with someone else for the first time and typically took people through the steps in as little as one to two days. Imagine what would happen if he'd waited six months or a year? His program, Alcoholics Anonymous, would never have gone anywhere.

A WORD OR TWO ON SPONSORS

For the duration of this book, I will refer to mentorship as "sponsorship" because it has been my experience that having a sponsor to assist you through the 12 Steps program is the only way to finally understand them. At the very least, you need someone to help you through the first four steps. If you don't have a sponsor at this point, feel free to consider me your sponsor while we work through the book and the steps together.

In my opinion, men shouldn't sponsor women and vice versa. It makes sense. Some things need to be talked about that are very sensitive in nature. Not to mention that if there is an attraction, then the motive for sponsorship may be flawed from the beginning.

I soon found that it became essential for me to find a good sponsor. Maybe because of some of the guys with long-term sobriety would say things like, "Cord, you won't ever get sober without a sponsor." Nonetheless, it was an uncomfortable process and one I didn't relish, but I recognized that like everyone else, I couldn't understand the 12 Steps as they were written and needed help.

Early on, I met a man I called Big John, who was 6'5" and at least 300lbs of solid muscle. I've never been around a larger man in my life and will always remember the first time I met him. He walked into an AA meeting just as they were starting to go around the room. He didn't even sit down before he commanded the space by calling out with a booming voice, "My name is John, and I am a real alcoholic! I did my 1st Step while serving 21 years in San Quentin State Prison. If any of you think you've had it worse off than me, come and see me after the meeting so I can explain a few things to you!" That's not exactly what he said, there were actually quite a few vulgarities as well.

After his dramatic entrance and announcement, he sat down directly across the table from me and stared straight at me with the coldest, hardest, steely red eyes I've ever seen. He looked a lot like the "Brawny Towel Man." He was spooky, but I was impressed! So when John got up to go to the bathroom, I turned to my friend, who was sitting next to me and said, "That's a guy I would want to have as my sponsor."

He said, "That's not a good idea. He's pretty rough and hard to be around most of the time. He doesn't sponsor anyone, but he definitely knows his stuff when it comes to the steps. Hell, he had 21 years to study it."

I said, "I'm going to talk with him after the meeting and ask him to consider being my sponsor." My friend wished me luck, and I said, "He's not going to get my goat!"

He said, "Really? "I think he just rode in on your goat!"

After the meeting, I approached John. He asked if I had done the 1st Step yet. I said yes and that I had been through the 12 Steps a few times. He asked me how I was managing to stay sober. I told him I was sober now but had slipped up a few times. He said, "There is no such thing as a slip-up brother. There is only a conscious decision to drink or use."

John then did something next that absolutely blew my me away. Something no one had done with me before. He pulled open his copy of *Alcoholics Anonymous*, turned to page 59, and handed it to me. He told me to read the 1st Step in the first person in my own words. I read: "I admit that I am powerless and that my life has become unmanageable."

He asked me what it meant to me? I said, "I am powerless when I have a drink of alcohol, or I use drugs. I crave more. I can't quit drinking. No matter what, I can't stop."

He said, "You couldn't be more wrong!"

He said, "You told me you had done your 1st Step? And I asked you how you have been managing to stay sober, and you said, 'you slipped up a few times.' The keywords here, Cord, are the ones you skipped over—'powerless' and 'unmanageable.' If you're managing to stay sober one day at a time or having some periods of sobriety. If you're one of those guys that think God isn't real or can't hear you. That if you continue to relapse over and over again, then you haven't completed your 1st Step as you said you have. And you certainly have never been through the 12 Steps! You don't recognize that you have no power. That the alcohol and drugs are managing you. That your life is a three-ring shit-show! Does this sound familiar to you?"

Wow, was this me! My life was a complete disaster. An unmanageable blob of chaos. I was going through life like a big ole wrecking ball. Bouncing and smashing my way from one disaster to the next. Obliterating every opportunity and every relationship. I couldn't get out of my own way!

John said, "You can't move past the first suggestion until you understand it, and you can't move past the next suggestion either until you fully understand that one, and so on. He said, would you like me to spend more time humiliating you further about your so-called knowledge of the next 11 steps? Or do you want to get real and honest with me about this issue?"

I said. "Okay, I'm an idiot, and I need help. Can you help me?"

John declined to sponsor me. He said that he didn't spend time with someone as new to sobriety and uncommitted to the process as me. But John did offer to be my friend and said I was welcome to talk with him about the steps anytime. I knew he didn't have any faith in me. I was trying to stay in control of something that was out of control.

He turned out to be an excellent friend and one that I learned a lot from, and in his own way, he did become a sponsor to me. He was the first guy that helped me understand what I was really dealing with. That my issue was a disease and a form of mental illness. I am grateful for him and the advice he has given me over the years. John, and others like him that I've worked with, I still consider sponsors, friends, and mentors. I often call on them for discussion and insight on issues in my life or someone I'm working with. This is what this is all about: one alcoholic/addict working with another.

I had another sponsor, Bill, who was a rough old cowboy—a real old-timer in AA. One of those guys who had been around since before there was hair, and he had great stories to tell.

One day we were sitting in his truck discussing the final step, and he was trying to help me understand the process. Bill believed that Step 12 meant I would work for him for free and be at his beck and call 24/7. You can imagine why I struggled with this concept. Bill became agitated as the conversation went on. When I said I wanted to stop to think and pray about this for a few days and then discuss it again after I had meditated on it, Bill freaked! He locked the doors and said, "You're not getting out of this truck until I tell you!"

It was unbelievable! I almost had to beat on poor old cowboy Bill just to get out of his truck! I told him I didn't want him as my sponsor. Bill took it very personally and told me he never wanted to talk to me again. It made me wonder if he had ever been through the steps himself? Someone who has actually been through the 12 Steps and had a spiritual awakening, experience, and psychic change wouldn't act that way.

The point is, you don't have an obligation to stick with a sponsor just because you are new to the process. And you can have more than one sponsor. You can have as many as you like if it helps. If your personality with one person doesn't mix, you have permission to fire them and move on. Just be honest about it and let them know. If they are true to their sobriety, honest themselves, and working this program like they should, they won't care about you moving on to find someone else. Sometimes personalities just clash. Sometimes people just can't get along for one reason or another. For the guys I sponsor, I hope they learn as much from what I did wrong as I did right, so it's a quicker process for them.

Because from the day I decided to become sober, I continued to suffer for seven more years. I quietly battled my addiction and hid it from my family. I might gain a little sobriety and then relapse. More times than I can count. I quietly went to AA meetings, NA, counseling, and therapists without the knowledge of my wife or family. I suffered, struggled, fought the compulsion to drink, and relapsed over and over again. I just couldn't find the answers I needed. Fighting the disease to the end, losing everything until I was defeated and broken. A story I will share with you later in the book.

One day, I found one man that knew the steps better than anyone I had ever met. I assumed he had studied them for years, read every book on the steps, taught workshops, and must have attended more 12-Step study meetings than anyone I had ever met. I quickly realized that this man had clearly had a spiritual awakening. He had changed his thinking through this process. He clearly had fully recovered from the disease of addiction. I asked him if he'd acquired his knowledge of the 12 Steps by spiritual awakening and a change in his thinking?

He said, "Nope! I had a sponsor take me through the steps in the same way they did in the 1940s. There is only one path to sobriety—through a spiritual awakening and a psychic change. Over time, people have come up with their own interpretation and meanings about the 12 Steps. That men, especially, develop a God complex and their own versions of the 12 Steps and how they should be taught. But why change something that is so simple and that works? Why fix something that isn't broken?"

"There is great importance of doing things exactly in the way they. The exact way that it was taught in the 1940s and 1950s by great men like Bill W., Doctor Bob, and the early pioneers of the AA movement because within these 12 Steps, there are specific promises to be gained that will take you to a life free from addiction."

It all made sense to me and sounded really good.

AWAKENING TO THE STEPS

You need to make a commitment to work on all 12 Steps to completion, and we'll discuss each one before moving on. If you complete the steps as they were taught initially, you'll find out a few things about yourself that you didn't know. You will experience a psychic change. You will experience a spiritual awakening that will take you further in your recovery from alcoholism or addiction then you've ever gone before. So while you're reading, and you see questions take a break and think about what you are reading and contemplate your own work and experiences as you have them.

Also, it's worth noting the following points:

The 4th Step is a written inventory of your character defects. When you get there, you will want the assistance of someone who has already been through it. Turn to your sponsor or ask someone to help you who have completed the steps. Ask this person to help you write to them if you need assistance. Or, if you are doing Step 4 for the first time, you'll be working through it with me, and I'll help you write it down by offering a wide range of examples. The point is this step does need to be written.

When I read *Alcoholics Anonymous* for the first time, I found some written instructions hard to understand and confusing, because of the era in which they were written, which is why it sometimes takes sponsors and newcomers so long to work through all steps.

You might also wonder why the authors devoted half of the book to Step 1. My understanding is because it is the foundation of sobriety. It's like building a commercial building or a home. The first thing you do when commencing construction is to lay down a solid foundation. If you take shortcuts or use cheap construction materials, guess what? You will always have trouble with the building's structure. You'll be continually going back to re-pour concrete, fix windows, walls, doors, etc., until ultimately, you are faced with going all the way back and establishing a solid foundation.

I didn't know this was the case when I started going through the 12 Steps, and I've experienced more relapses than I can count and been through multiple treatment programs. One might think my history in this process is full of pathetic and failed attempts at sobriety. I went in and out of AA meetings, counseling, and treatment programs for years, trying to find my way. I went to a lot of AA and NA meetings. Sometimes while intoxicated. I just couldn't stay sober. I couldn't stop drinking and using. I thought there was something very wrong with the 12 Step program.

Looking back, there were a few things I overlooked. Little things such as finding a sponsor to help me with the 12 Steps, reading the Big Book, Narcotics Anonymous, doing the 12 Steps to completion, reading other publications on addiction and alcoholism, building a relationship with a higher power—or God as I choose to call it—and sharing the message of hope with someone else. Yeah, I guess in hindsight, I overlooked a few things.

You see, I came to sobriety, kicking and screaming. I came in with a big ego, and I thought I was smarter than every one of you. I was better than you and was convinced that I wasn't an alcoholic or an addict like you. I was the guy walking in late to every meeting I ever went to, just to make sure you knew I had arrived. The one sitting in the back and usually leaving early to make sure you knew that I really didn't need to be there. The guy pushing all my views on everyone about what the 12 Steps were all about. I had a lot of opinions, and I wanted you to hear every single one of them. And I had a big ego. I had it all figured out and didn't need any one's help.

I was the guy in the meeting that was standing on my soapbox, pontificating about experiences that I had never had because I hadn't completed the 12 Steps myself. I was telling you someone else's experiences. I had opinions on the steps that were better than anyone else because I thought I was smarter than you. I didn't need a sponsor. I didn't need to work through the steps like everyone else. I had it all under control.

The only time I ever had any humility was on those days when I would walk to the front of the room with my head down to pick up another 24-hour chip and a hug after a relapse. But as soon as you would all applaud me for my stupidity, cheer me on and say, "Attaboy Cord!" I was right back to the same ole me. "Yeah, I know the 12 Steps, I've had my spiritual awakening, I've done my Step 4. Just ask me about making amends, I'll tell you all about that. I know God. You want my opinion? I'll give them all to you!" Then I'd relapse a few weeks later and start it all over again. I was hopelessly pathetic.

There was a period before I got sober that I didn't have a home or job. I had lost everything. I didn't have a car. I lived in a small hotel room. I did anything to survive, including begging for just enough money to buy another bottle and a night in a hotel. No one wanted to be anywhere near me. I was like a lightning rod for bad luck. I couldn't relate to any one of those people in the meetings. I had nothing. I wasn't like them. The point is that because of the 12 Steps and the promises, my life began to change.

BEFORE WE BEGIN . . .

For the purpose of this book, I will be referring to alcoholism because that is primarily who I am. I am a grateful recovered alcoholic/addict, however. In my opinion, the 12 Steps apply to all addictions and can be used in daily life as a method of overcoming anything. I've also used the 12 Steps to help me through many issues in my life besides alcoholism, including personal relationships, depression, anxiety, mental health issues, even smoking.

I smoked cigarettes for years. Someone once said to me. "The cigarette is doing all the smoking, you're just the sucker behind it!" I never really understood why I smoked, except that I really liked smoking. I hated the smell, the hassle of finding a place to smoke, and the cost.

I always wanted to quit. I tried many times throughout those years unsuccessfully. When I fully understood the 12 Steps and the promises found within them, I simply applied what I knew from the 12 Steps to cigarettes, threw them away, and never picked them up again. Actually never craved them after the day that I did that. Kind of cool, isn't it? There is still the one issue I have with chocolate, but let's save that for another time, okay?

The point is that you can use these 12 Steps to overcome anything in your life once you understand them. I personally believe that the steps must have been divinely given to the authors that wrote them. There is a simple proven plan of action found within them and a promise that will set you free. Free from addiction. Free from the struggles you go through in your life on this earth. If you complete the 12 Steps as outlined in the following pages of this book, I promise you that you will find serenity, freedom, and peace as have thousands of men and women before you.

For the young people reading this book. I admire you for working on the 12 Steps early on in your life. I wish someone had taken me through them when I was your age. My life would have been so much happier in my early adult years if I had been free from my addictions.

Have you ever heard anyone say, "Our youth don't stand a chance?" Really?! They have a better chance of overcoming their addictions using these 12 Steps than anyone on this planet. They are fantastic to be around. Case in point. The movement of Young People in Alcoholics Anonymous (YPAA) is more significant than you would imagine.

At the 1960 AA Convention, Bill W. noted that the age of new members was much lower than when he and Dr. Bob founded AA 25 years earlier. In a letter to ICYPAA dated June 15, 1969, Bill W. wrote that he was inspired by the fact that the AA in the future would be safe because of our youth.

I've attended many YPAA (Young People in Alcoholics Anonymous) conferences over the past years and have always been impressed by the numbers of young people in this group. These conferences aren't attended by hundreds but thousands of young sober individuals having the time of their lives. I've never witnessed so many of our youth in one place without the presence of drugs and alcohol. Some will say that the movement of YPAA is much larger than that of AA.

I believe that all addictions are a disease and are a form of mental disorder. I repeat: It doesn't matter whether you suffer from alcohol, drugs, sex, eating disorder, anxiety, depression, gambling, adrenaline, cigarettes, or compulsive hoarding. They are all addictive mental disorders and behaviors and can be cured through the use of the 12 Steps.

HAPPINESS IS NOT
A PERSON, PLACE,
OR THING.
IT IS A STATE
OF MIND.

CHAPTER 1

NO POWER

We are not human beings having a spiritual experience;
we are spiritual beings having a human experience.

—PIERRE TEILHARD DE CHARDIN

The first time I went through the 12 Steps with a sponsor, he told me to have fun and try to find humor in myself and my past experiences. He said, "Cord, don't take yourself too seriously, okay? After all, you are the joke!" True story. He also gave me a worksheet, which really helped me understand the process and get through the first suggestion. So I'd also like to start by taking you through the same exercise now. This isn't a test of whether you're ready for the 1st Step but will assist you in understanding a little better where you are at right now.

Read through the following 10 statements, and answer TRUE or FALSE to each one:

- If I'm planning to stop drinking or using, all I have to do is not drink one day at a time.
  TRUE/FALSE

- Once I complete the steps, I will have a relationship with my higher power or God.
  TRUE/FALSE

- Once I understand God, I will be free from my addiction.
  TRUE/FALSE

- My purpose in sobriety is to get back to my life and family.
  TRUE/FALSE

- There are many different ways I can work this.
  TRUE/FALSE

- My sobriety is my greatest possession.
  TRUE/FALSE

- It takes a long time to recover from addictions.
  TRUE/FALSE

- The steps are not required, only suggested.
  TRUE/FALSE

- Going to meetings and not drinking is vital to my recovery.
  TRUE/FALSE

- Our collective suffering is what holds us, alcoholics and addicts, together.
  TRUE/FALSE

Take note of your answers and keep them somewhere safe because we'll be revisiting these 10 TRUE or FALSE statements later in the book. You might be surprised to see how much your answers have changed.

I still enjoy attending AA and NA meetings because I always come away with something I can hold on to. Someone had something to say that I needed to hear that day. If nothing else, the next time you attend a meeting, or if it is your first one, take a look at what is written on the walls of almost every meeting place. Notice that they all have what is known as the "12 promises." The first time I read them, I didn't understand what they meant or why they were there, but they gave me hope. I hope that by the time you finish going through the 12 Steps in this book with me, you'll fully understand how they can assist you in daily life and sobriety. The 12 promises are also found within the first few paragraphs of the Big Book and are read at the end of every meeting.

In general, these promises tell us that we will be amazed before we are halfway through the 12 Steps. That we will come to know freedom and happiness. We will not regret our past mistakes. Through these steps, we will find peace and serenity. Because of our suffering, we will see how our experiences can benefit others. We will stop feeling useless. Our selfishness will fade away. Our outlook on life will change. We will no longer fear issues of money or people. Things that used to baffle us, no longer will. We will finally understand that God is doing for us what we were never capable of doing for ourselves.

The promises will come to you if you follow the 12 Steps. It worked for me, and I know it will work for you too. I believe these promises are nothing more than statements of hope. Wouldn't you agree?

WHAT DO YOU BELIEVE, RIGHT NOW?

Most of you will have heard or been told that addiction isn't something you can recover from. That once you have identified addiction as something that you suffer from, you'll live with it for the rest of your life. You may have also been told that you will always be fighting addiction and will never be cured of it. Always be in recovery. That now that you have admitted to addiction, you will be chained to a life of daily meetings, AA, NA, sponsors, and never-ending step work, or you will die from your disease. Sounds bleak, doesn't it?

As we begin, I want to call your attention to something I found inside the front cover of the Big Book. It reads that this is the story of how thousands of men and women have recovered from alcoholism. A pretty bold statement, wouldn't you agree? It doesn't say anything about non-stop meetings, never-ending Step work, staying sober only one day at a time, needing to call a sponsor every day, endless reading, asking God to keep you sober just for today. Being in recovery for the rest of your life. Never to be cured of your addictions. NO, it just says:

We "recovered" a.k.a. "cured."

Even if you don't believe this right now, isn't it worth exploring? After all, other diseases are curable. Why should addiction be any different? So go ahead and ask yourself: "If I was diagnosed with cancer, diabetes, cystic fibrosis, or Alzheimer's today, would I seek a cure or accept the idea that I was just going to have to live with the disease, fighting my recovery from it until the bitter end?"

Would you accept that something like cancer can't be cured? Or would you research, educate yourself, attend support groups, seek treatment until you found the right answer for a cure? Why is addiction different from any other disease or mental health issue? Why would you ever believe that it is incurable? Is it because that's what they tell you at meetings? That's what a sponsor told you? Is it because you heard this from an individual who has no formal education, professional license, or experience to be able to diagnosis such a terminal disease? Are you really going to believe this nonsense?

After I decided to stop using alcohol and drugs, it took me another seven long years of suffering to find the answers to these questions, until one day I actually read what it said on the inside front cover of the Big Book. What I had been reading during those years of suffering, was actually just a story of how thousands and men and women had recovered from alcoholism. How they had been cured. At that moment, I felt a tremendous amount of relief and hope. It should give you hope too.

What I found in the process of going through the 12 Steps was that each of them, except the 1st Step, has specific promises of hope written within it. Step 1 is a process of admitting to yourself where you are at today. But there are a total of 12 specific promises found within the 12 Steps, and we'll explore each one in the following chapters.

Throughout the 12 Steps, you'll also see some statements come up, which we'll pause to discuss. Each of these statements gave me a lot of hope, and I'd like you to think of them as "promises of hope." Promises that we can realize if we do the work and complete the steps.

I can promise you that it works. It worked me, for my sponsor, and thousands of men and women before us as stated in the beginning of the Big Book. So why wouldn't it work for you? I can offer you this promise. If you go all the way through the steps, do the work as suggested, and then decide you are better off drinking and using, I will gladly refund your misery . . .

CRAVINGS AND ALLERGIES

So let's dig into those promises of hope by looking at the section titled "The Doctor's Opinion" in the Big Book. Here, Dr. Silkworth writes about how an alcoholic should be free from physical addiction. That craving is not a mental issue but a physical one. An obsession of the mind, not the body. When I read this, I could see how it might be right. Addiction is an obsession of the mind, not the body. The body experiences a craving, sickness, withdrawal, and pain; the mind doesn't. Therefore, craving can't be a mental issue.

The authors expertly explore the physical aspects and mental obsession of alcoholism as discrete topics over 40 or so pages. Dr. Silkworth wrote that after an alcoholic takes their first drink of the day, the phenomenon of craving takes over, and nothing else, including important meetings, mattered after that. He did a masterful job of explaining the meaning of "craving" as a physical, not a mental issue. This means it's impossible to experience a craving unless you put alcohol or drugs in your body. Dr. Silkworth goes on to describes his belief that the effect of alcohol on chronic alcoholics is the manifestation of an allergy. Meaning that an alcoholic has an abnormal reaction to alcohol when they drink, and this reaction is an allergy.

As we go through these steps, I would ask that you have an open mind. That you don't assume you're an alcoholic or an addict just because you are reading my book. Instead, I urge you to use this time to discover the truth about your own experiences as we walk through the Steps together. I want you to discover the truth about your own personal experiences on your own.

I say this because I believe we all have addictions or issues of some kind. As I said before, we will be referring to the words alcoholism or addictions only because that is my experience. I ask that you replace my words with your issues if you will, to help you complete the steps so that you have your personal experience. However, our 1st Step is to find out who you really are so you can identify what to do next. This is crucial because unless you're very clear about your own experiences with drugs, alcohol, or other obsessions or addictions, then you won't be able to share your experiences with someone else who really needs your help?

WHAT'S NORMAL?

So let's talk about what Dr. Silkworth meant when he labeled alcoholism an allergy. When I first went through this with a sponsor that really understood this concept, he asked me to go through the book and turn the things I was experiencing into questions, such as "Do you have an abnormal reaction to alcohol when you drink?" But before I could answer that question, I needed to know what an "abnormal reaction" was, and my sponsor explained it in the following way.

"You know how abnormal alcoholics are when they can't remember what happened the night before or where they had been or with whom? Have you ever noticed how alcoholics can never remember what they've said to you over the phone the night before? The drunk calls at 2 a.m. and then again at 10 a.m. the next morning in confusion and asking, 'Are you and I okay?' For most people, this type of behavior would scare the hell out of them."

Ask yourself: *When I drink, do I have a normal or abnormal reaction? Is everything normal and fun when I drink? Can I take or leave it? Stop whenever I want? Or do I regret the things I do when I'm drinking?*

WANTING MORE

Dr. Silkworth also wrote that the phenomenon of craving is limited to certain people and doesn't "ever" occur in the average tempered drinker. But what is craving? The definition is "a powerful desire for something." My sponsor asked me the same question when he said, "When you drink, do you have a craving for more alcohol?"

I answered, "I don't know, but I want more."

This is precisely what a craving is! If every time you drink alcohol, you want more, wouldn't you call that a craving? And at this point, it's also worth saying that *Alcoholics Anonymous* was written for alcoholism, not for other addictions. However, you will find that everything in the book also applies to every addiction, mental health crisis, or issue in your life. As we continue, please read it in that manner and apply it to your own circumstances.

Dr. Silkworth wrote, "NEVER" occurs in the average tempered drinker. When I read this sentence, it became clear to me that I was an alcoholic. It doesn't show me the drama, chaos, fear, and devastation I created when I drank. Just the simplicity of the fact that when I drank alcohol, everything about me changed and was completely abnormal.

Back when the authors first shared their messages of hope, they spoke about their inner experiences. About drinking alcohol and wanting more. About abnormal reactions to alcohol, guilt, shame, and regret. About how they would go to a hospital and dry out and then drink again and again. About the hopelessness, fears, depression, and anxiety. The feeling that there was no meaning in life.

If you have been to an AA meeting, how many have you attended and listened to a lot of meaningless drama? Where there are a lot of so-called drunk-a-logs being shared?

Imagine you're brand new to the AA concept, at your first meeting, and looking for some form of hope. But standing in the back of the room, a guy is going on and on about his miserable, pathetic life. He's talking about the horrible years he spent in prison. How he got sober in solitary confinement after hitting another prisoner or prison guard. He talks about all the DUIs, drug busts, cops, arrests, courtrooms, jail time, over and over again. He talks about how hard it was on probation and the thousands of dollars in legal fees and court fines he's paid. How his wife left him, and his children hate his guts. How he filed for bankruptcy and lost everything. How he is homeless, broken, defeated, and alone. And then ends with "But hey? I'm grateful to be sober just for today."

As a newcomer, sitting in that room, feeling fearful and confused, and this is what I hear at my first meeting. A place where I thought I could find a little shred of hope. I'm thinking to myself: "Who are these people? I've never been to prison. I've never experienced solitary confinement. I would never hit a prisoner or prison guard. I don't have any DUIs. I've never been arrested. I've never even talked to a cop or been to a courtroom in my life. I still have a job. My wife hasn't left me yet. My kids are worried about their dad, but I know they love me. I've never filed for bankruptcy. I'm not homeless, broken, defeated, and alone. I just know I have a big problem on my hands, and I can't seem to stop!"

So perhaps not surprising when that newcomer then thinks, "If this is what alcoholism looks like, maybe I'm not an alcoholic. I'm not like that loser running his mouth up there," and so gets up and walks out. He leaves the one place that should have been safe. The place he or she needed most at that very moment in their life. A place where all of us are supposed to be doing our job and sharing a message of hope. Not our notes on misery and despair!

In this situation, we just lost this person, and they don't even know what alcoholism is yet. We never allowed them to find out who they really are. Through our own ignorance and irresponsibility, we just took the only fighting chance they had. Drama creates a lot of distance and confusion, rather than understanding and situations that we can relate to. That stores of trauma are things that should be shared over a cup of coffee outside of AA, not inside the meeting rooms.

My sponsor taught me to always carry a message of hope and encouragement for newcomers when I went to a meeting. And I should be there for that one purpose. To identify someone who needs to hear that there is hope and talk to them about it. He said if you feel the need to tell someone how pathetic and meaningless your life is, do it in a coffee shop, not in an AA meeting.

IT'S DIFFERENT FOR US: WE HAVE AN ALLERGY

To go back to craving.

Ask yourself: *When I drink alcohol, do I crave more?*

Dr. Silkworth writes that it "never" occurs in the average tempered drinker. Let's say out of 20 to 30 times that you drink, you only experience craving half the time. Does that make you an alcoholic? Most likely, according to Dr. Silkworth. Because he said "it never" occurs in the average tempered drinker. He doesn't say, "sometimes." He doesn't say "once in a while." He says, "NEVER"!

What separates me from a non-alcoholic has nothing to do with the drama alcohol brings me. It has nothing to do with how many DUIs or arrests I've had. Nothing to do with my divorce, wrecking my car, jail sentences, courtrooms, losing my job and filing for bankruptcy, heart failure, cirrhosis of the liver, esophagitis, internal bleeding, and stints in the mental hospital. It has to with one thing and only one thing: the phenomenon of craving. When I put alcohol in my body, I have an abnormal reaction to it: my face gets flushed, I break out in hives on my chest and neck, and I want more. I have an allergy.

How many times have you gone out with people who drink when you haven't? And you've watched them drink one or two drinks and then say, "I better stop or slow down." I've witnessed this many times, and I can't relate to it. Have you ever watched someone order a glass of wine or beer and then not finish it? Are you nuts? In my world, that is absurd. That's just getting started.

Over the years, I've had friends question me about this issue and make comments like, "Cord, we'd ask you to go out with us if you weren't such a damn lush. Why can't you just have a few drinks with us and leave it alone?"

A very close friend of mine was dying from cancer, and I spent a lot of time with him during this time. We had a lot of discussions about this issue of mine. At one time, Roger was my business partner and closest friend and someone I drank with almost daily. He could never understand why I couldn't just stop when he did. He was always composed after drinks while I was a sloppy mess.

One day I went to his apartment to see how he was doing. We talked for a while about the good times, and he offered me a drink. If we could have one last drink together. I told him I couldn't. He said, "I don't understand. You've been sober for years. One glass of wine isn't going to set you off, is it?

I jokingly replied, "No. But the next 15 to 20 after that one will . . . and I've things to do later this year, my friend." He asked again why it was so different for me. I told him. "It's simple. For me, it is the phenomenon of craving."

He asked, "What do you mean?"

I replied, "If I have even one drink, I experience an uncontrollable craving for more alcohol, and there is no way for me to stop."

Dr. Silkworth wrote about how alcoholics are irritable, restless, and discontent unless they can have more alcohol. He talks about how they see other people drink without issue. How the phenomenon of craving takes over, and they can't stop until they pass out, wake up, and swear not to do it again.

Ask yourself: *Am I irritable, restless, and discontent?*

Do you start to see that this also applies to sobriety? For me, I need to find things in sobriety to take the place of drinking, or I could be back in the same situation as when I was drinking all those years. Irritable, restless, and discontent, which always leads me back to drinking. There is a lot of peace, calm, and hope in the 12 Steps.

I was one of those drinkers who kept my hard alcohol hidden all around the house because I was always terrified about running out. Or that my wife and kids would see me drinking too much. I would hide it. Tell them I was only drinking wine and then sneak a vodka from the bottle that I'd hidden in a closet. And it never really mattered to me that I passed out by 9 p.m. every night. It didn't matter that the phone, water, or power was turned off. It didn't matter that my wife said, "I'm leaving you if you don't stop." None of this mattered because I would get my alcohol, take that first big drink and say, "Ahhh . . . You see. Everything is okay. Nothing to worry about now. Life is good!"

The irony is I have the same experience in sobriety. I know that if I follow the Steps, deep down in my heart, no matter what, as long as I'm sober, I will be happy and everything will be okay.

CHANGING THE WAY YOU THINK

Getting back to where we were. Dr. Silkworth goes on to say how these episodes are repeated over and over, and unless the person can experience an entire physic change, there will be very little hope of recovery. My personal experience in reading this is that there needs to be a change in the way I think.

Ask yourself: *Do I have the power to just change the way I think about alcohol and drinking without any help?*

If you could just magically change the way you think, why would you need the 12 Steps, a higher power, or a sponsor to talk to? Why not just quit? Because if you could, you would have already done this.

Ask yourself: *Unless I am willing to experience an entire physic change, is there little hope for my recovery? Am I willing to admit this?*

Are you willing to consider that you need something other than human power to experience an essential "physic change"? The authors wrote that unless the entire physic change has occurred, there is very little hope for recovery at all. No human power can make this happen.

Ask yourself: *Can a sponsor or spouse make the needed physic change in me? Can my wife or children or family? Can money, house, car, boat, or clothes make an entire physic change in me?*

If the answer is NO, then it strongly suggests something more than human is needed to cause an "entire physic change." Are you willing to consider this?

I read an example of this in "Bill's Story" in the Big Book. On a bleak November day, in 1934, Bill Wilson's old friend Ebby T. came to visit. Bill was sitting in his kitchen, drinking gin. Ebby knocks on Bill's door, and when he answered, he notices immediately that Ebby is sober. Bill hasn't seen this guy for a few years. Bill offers Ebby a drink, and he refuses. Bill inquires what's changed? Ebby talks of finding his way through religion. Ebby tells Bill that God had done for him what he couldn't do for himself.

Bill knows that there is something different about Ebby and tries to figure out where Ebby got the knowledge and power to stop drinking. Bill wonders if this power originated from within Ebby and then quickly surmises that it hasn't. He concludes that there was no more power in Ebby than there was in himself at that very minute. At this moment, Bill W. realizes that he has no power, and this is the very essence of Step 1: No human power is enough to stop me from drinking, using, or to fix life's issues.

As I read to this point in the *Big Book*, I realized that the authors had spent over half of their book, 43 pages, just to get this one simple point across. The realization:

I have no power to stop drinking on my own.

I always thought that Step 1 was about not drinking. That it was about just staying sober one day at a time. What I found out was that Step 1 had nothing to do with drinking alcohol or using drugs. Think about it: If Step 1 is about not using, then we can skip the next 11 Steps and just stop! At this point, what became clear regarding my alcoholism and the disease of addiction was this: Until I found the 12 Steps and had a spiritual awakening, I was going to drink alcohol and use drugs no matter what!

You see, I don't have the power not to drink without the help of the 12 Steps and a daily reprieve contingent on the maintenance of my spiritual condition. I didn't start going to AA because I was court-ordered. I didn't go to treatment seven different times because I wanted to stop drinking. By the time I truly got through the 12 Steps, I had nothing. I was emotionally, spiritually, financially, and physically broken. All I wanted was to stop suffering the way I had done for so long. I came in because I had no power to do this alone.

Ask yourself: *If I could drink all I wanted every day and there were no consequences, would I still be drinking? I need to consider whether I came to where I am today because I really want to stop drinking or because I want to stop the suffering and pain?*

For me, I wasn't persuaded I wanted to stop drinking. I just knew I wanted the pain to stop. I knew I wanted to stop the loneliness, depression, anxiety, fear, and sadness. But I didn't know for sure if I wanted to stop drinking. In fact, stopping was the last thing on my mind. If there were no consequences to my drinking, believe you me, I would be sitting on a beach somewhere with a Mai Tai in my hand! So if anyone ever says, "I want to stop drinking," they're probably lying! Anyone who drinks alcohol likes to drink. They like socializing with friends and having fun. They like the euphoria that alcohol gives them. They like the feeling. That "Ahhh, now everything's going to be okay" feeling. They just don't like the consequences.

For a long time, I would quietly go to AA meetings while I was still drinking. I would try not to talk to anyone because I was often drunk. It seemed pointless, I know, but I kept going and didn't understand why. In hindsight, I can see that it was because I wanted to stop the pain and suffering. I'd had enough of that. But I wasn't convinced that I had no power. The reality was that I had no power!

If you're like me, you probably came to this point in your life with one specific goal: To learn how to not drink or use one day at a time. To satisfy a court order, angry wife, disappointed children, or to keep a job. And that is precisely what I was told at every meeting. I was going to learn the techniques and get the tools I needed. I was going to get more information. I was convinced that was all I needed—more information.

I learned all about it. I learned all about the progression of my disease. What denial and mental obsession mean. I could tell you where all the meetings were in my area and at what times. But I couldn't stop drinking no matter what. The issue was I had no power. No power to stop drinking and stay sober. I wanted to be sober, but I couldn't stop.

In Bill's story, the authors wrote about having no power.

Ask yourself: *Do I have the power to stop drinking once I start, and the phenomenon of craving has kicked in? Can I control the mental obsession once I've taken my first drink?*

I hadn't figured out precisely what Step 1 was all about. I knew what it said. I admitted that I had no power over alcohol—that my life had become unmanageable. But I had no clue what this really meant. I thought it was just about telling someone I was a drunk! So ask yourself another couple of questions.

Ask yourself: *If I have no power to stop drinking, if I have no power to control the obsession once I start drinking, then just how manageable is my life? Is my life manageable, or is it that three-ring shit show of chaos and confusion we talked about earlier?*

CAN YOU TAKE IT OR LEAVE IT?

Before we drill down into this idea any further, I want to let you know that when I first understood what I'm about to share, it had a profound and immediate impact on me—one I will never forget. I finally figured out who I was, and because of that, it ultimately led to my sobriety.

Addiction is a real disease. Just like cancer, heart disease, or diabetes. If you were diagnosed with lung cancer today, would you seek help? Would you find out more about your disease and how to stop smoking, or would you just keep doing what you have always done?

Sometimes, we have to start with the basics of understanding who we really are and what we really have before we can move in the right direction and start asking others for help. Okay, let's explore some more.

The authors of the Big Book wrote about moderate drinkers. How they have little trouble in giving up alcohol entirely if they have a good enough reason to stop. That moderate drinkers can take it or leave it.

Stop now . . .

Ask yourself: *Can I take or leave alcohol?*

If you can, then you're probably a moderate drinker and not an alcoholic. The authors also wrote that there are certain types of hard drinkers. That they may have a habit badly enough to gradually impair themselves physically and mentally. That they may die a few years before their time. If these people have sufficient reason—for example, health, falling in love, change of environment, or the warning of a doctor—they can stop or moderate, but that they may find it difficult and may at some point need medical attention.

Ask yourself: *Is there sufficient enough reason for me to stop or moderate at this point in my life? Am I just a hard drinker?*

I always thought that this is who I was. I would always tell myself that I work hard, so I deserve to play even harder. I remember, at one point, my wife telling me that I needed to stop drinking and seek help, or she would leave and take our daughter with her. I said, "Okay, bye." I couldn't let that get in the way of my drinking. I needed alcohol more than anything.

In hindsight, watching my marriage and family fall apart should have been a pretty good indication that I wasn't just a "hard drinker." Was that normal or abnormal and unmanageable? So what's the definition of the real alcoholic?

I remember early on in my sobriety, I heard something at a meeting for the first time when a guy spoke up and said his name and then added, "I'm a real alcoholic."

I remember thinking, "What an asshole! We are all alcoholics here, why would you say that? Why else would we be here if we weren't?"

What I didn't know at that time was what I was about to discover because, as the authors of the Big Book wrote, an alcoholic may start off as a moderate drinker. I knew a lot of people in my life that drank more than me, and the only difference was they weren't alcoholics.

We read that a real alcoholic may or may not become a continuous hard drinker, but at some stage of their drinking career, they begin to lose all control of the amount of their consumption, once they start to drink. Meaning one drink is never enough.

This is what separates a moderate or hard drinker and a real alcoholic. Once I take just one sip of alcohol, I lose all control. I have no power to stop. I can't take it or leave it. I can't stop when sufficient reason is present. I can't stop, no matter what, until catastrophic things happen in my life.

I have to be clear about this for myself. If I have clarity about the phenomenon of craving, who I am, and my experience with this, then I can help someone else become clear too. So I don't profess to know who is and who isn't an alcoholic. That is a decision you need to make for yourself. But I am very clear about my own experience with this and can share it with someone else.

Ask yourself: *Am I a moderate drinker? Am I a hard drinker? Can I stop drinking if sufficient reason is present? Am I a real alcoholic?*

I've sponsored people who have stopped drinking or gone through treatment to stop who, when I ask them, "Are you a real alcoholic?" They say yes, but when I ask them how they know, they say it's because that's what they've been told at a treatment center. I've also had people come into my treatment center addicted to heroin, cocaine, or other drugs, who say they aren't alcoholic but addicted to drugs. And, after going through the 12 Steps with me, say, "Cord, I figured out who I am? I am a real alcoholic."

I've also experienced just the opposite. Many come in for drug addiction treatment but believe being sober is defined by not using their drug of choice while continuing to drink alcohol. These are usually the same people I see at meetings taking a 24-hour newcomer chip over and over again. People who come in and out of sobriety. They are just like I was. In and out. I would get 30 days, 60 days, a couple of months, and then use it again.

The reason this happens is that, like me, every time they open their mouth to say, "I am not an alcoholic," they are lying—just as I once did. A drug is a drug. It doesn't really matter whether it's alcohol, tobacco, cocaine, opiates, heroin, meth, or benzodiazepines. The principle is the same. Looking at myself, I admitted that alcohol was my drug of choice, but still, I was an everything-else user. I would take anything that would make me high. And there was never enough once I started, and the phenomenon of craving was present.

For me, sobriety is not using any drug at all. Not even tobacco. After all, nicotine is a drug. For others who believe they are just addicted to a specific drug and not alcohol, they have their own experiences with who they are. They sometimes find a different meeting to attend that works better for them. Maybe they go to NA instead of AA because it fits better with who they are and their own experiences and situation. It is crucial to be clear about our own experiences and situations.

The Big Book talks about "mental obsession" and how the alcoholic's main problem is in their mind, rather than in their body. If this is true, then alcohol is only a symptom of my problem. The main problem is in our thinking, which makes this an excellent time to look at your own experiences in life.

Ask yourself: *Was my thinking obscured or clear before starting the 12 Steps?*

SURRENDERING TO THE TRUTH

I know my thinking was obscured. In fact, my confused and cloudy mind has caused me more pain, more suffering, more financial, and legal trouble than anything else. This is why I could relate when the authors wrote that most alcoholics, for reasons they don't understand, lose the power of choice when they take the first drink of alcohol. I can relate to this, can you?

Stop and turn this into a question . . .

Ask yourself: *When I drink alcohol, do I lose the power to choose?*

I hear this in meetings, "I choose to not drink today." If it were that easy, if I could choose, then would I need the AA or the 12 Steps or a sponsor or a higher power to be sober? I wouldn't. I'd just not drink!

Years ago, my brother took up drinking wine, which quickly developed into a daily routine. He said that at some point, he simply chose to stop because it was starting to interfere with his work and family. Does he sound like a real alcoholic? I think not. If I had the power to do this, I would. So why is it hard for me to stop? I read that our so-called willpower is, for the most part, nonexistent. That we can't remember clearly, the amount of suffering and humiliation, we have had in our past to keep us from taking that first drink.

In other words, remembering how bad it was for me isn't enough to stop me from drinking. That no matter how much education I have, how much suffering and pain I go through, or the probable loss of my family, friends, and business, and potential health problems will not keep me sober. Nothing will keep me from drinking.

It is absolutely imperative to my survival that I admit to my innermost self that I have no power once I start drinking. That I surrender to the fact that there is absolutely nothing that I can do to keep myself sober. That I am going to drink no matter what, once I start! That I don't have any defense against the first drink.

Ask yourself: *Do I have any defense against the first drink?*

Again the authors emphasize that alcoholics have no power once they take the first drink. That, as an alcoholic, I don't have a defense. I know it has always been that way with me. I need power more than anything to keep me from drinking. I need something greater than me. A higher power. Real power!

I always thought that going to AA or treatment would give me the tools to stop drinking. That's what I'd always been told. I didn't understand at the time that what I really needed was to experience my 1st Step. I had never done it before. I needed to surrender and to concede to the fact that I had no power. I needed to admit, just as it is written in the 12 Steps: I am "power-less" once I drink alcohol. Powerless against the phenomenon of craving once I take that first drink.

As a result of having a 1st Step experience and making an admission and conceding to my innermost self about who I really was, I was able to surrender and find a power greater than me. Once I surrendered, I gained a burning desire to seek out power. Real power!

Until I had this experience on my own, I had no desire to seek out a power greater than me. Consider this. If I already have the power I need to stop drinking and stay sober, then do I really need a 1st Step experience? I should be able to just quit anytime I want. This is the very reason why the authors spend 43 pages of their book on Step 1. Clue: it is the most important one.

GAINING SELF-UNDERSTANDING

The 12 Steps help identify whether we are unable to drink or we moderate. The question for us is how to stop altogether, let alone moderate. Assuming we really want to stop. The issue is whether a person can quit entirely on a nonspiritual basis based on the lack of power to choose whether to drink or not.

Ask yourself: *Do I believe I can stop drinking on a nonspiritual basis, using my own willpower?*

If not, then you might be having the same experience that thousands of men and women have had at this point. The same experience I had.

Ask yourself: *If I can't quit on a nonspiritual basis, then I have lost the power to choose whether I will or will not drink, haven't I?*

Early in my journey, I had several sponsors trying to help me find the answers I needed. I thought that a sponsor was someone to just get information from in the morning or at night. Someone who was supposed to talk me out of drinking. None of them were successful in helping me to understand this simple proven plan except for one.

I met a man who impressed me with his knowledge of the 12 Steps, and I asked him if he would sponsor me and take me through the Steps. He asked me if I had been through Step 1 before. "Of course," I told him. I had been through all of the steps several times and with several different sponsors and didn't feel it necessary to do it all over again.

However, with this guy, it was different. I will never forget his next question: "Cord, be honest with me. Can you choose to not drink today?"

At that point in my life, I honestly couldn't. We wouldn't need all of this if it were that simple. So how about you?

Ask yourself: *Can I simply choose to not drink today?*

I had to explore the idea that if I am really an alcoholic, then I believe there is no simple solution for me. I believe life has become impossible. I have passed the point of no return, and no alternatives or humanitarian aid can help me. That my only decision at this point is to go on to the bitter end or accept spiritual help. I found the answer in Step 1. The authors are clear that there are only two alternatives: Keep drinking until death or seek spiritual help. There is no middle-of-the-road solution for real alcoholics. Explore this within yourself.

Ask yourself: *What will happen if I seek out a middle-of-the-road solution?*

What I mean by the middle of the road is to be one of those guys you see at AA meetings every week and never misses one. This is a man who comes to the same meeting every single day. Shares at the same meeting every single day and says the same exact thing every single day, proclaiming that all you need to do to stay sober is read the Big Book, get a sponsor, come to a meeting every day and ask God to keep you sober just for today. Doesn't talk about the Steps or doing the work at all. I must consider that this is someone who may be trying a middle-of-the-road solution.

So what if you keep going to meetings but do none of the work that it takes? What if you never seek out a sponsor? Never experience the 12 Steps or promises? Never find a higher power. Never have a spiritual awakening or physic change. Will you stay sober?

I've tried all of this. I went to meetings every day for the longest time. I didn't want a sponsor. I was the guy in the back of the room, not getting involved. Not sharing my experiences because I had never had one. I hadn't done the work necessary to have my own experience. It didn't work out for me. I drank again and again. And it wasn't until I actually completed the 12 Steps and had my own spiritual awakening, my own experiences, that I was able to be free. Free from myself. Free from the compulsion to drink or use. *Are you willing to do the work needed for freedom from drugs or alcohol? How free do you want to be?*

MANAGING THE UNMANAGEABLE

Let's explore the issue of unmanageability.

Ask yourself: *What is the most insane thing I have ever done either while I was drinking or sober?*

I'm not talking about the obvious DUIs, arrests, going to court, falling down in public, jail time, making an ass of yourself in public, yelling at a wife, child, or friend. I am talking about something much more insane than this.

I'll share mine. The most stupid and insane thing I did was

when I was four years into sobriety. Cruising along, staying sober, and going to meetings. Sponsoring guys and working the 12 Steps. At that time, I was the happiest I had been in years. I was Mr. AA. Had the rings, hats, t-shirts with "RECOVERY" printed on them. I was a chairperson at a meeting every day and secretary at another nightly meeting. I had it all under control.

One day I was out to dinner with a friend at a convention in Las Vegas. He was having a glass of wine and asked me if I would like one. My mind said, "I think I can have a glass of wine today. I can handle it."

Does this sound insane to you? Does this look like a life that is manageable or unmanageable? Is this normal or abnormal? After years of chasing answers to find sobriety. After going in and out of seven different treatment programs and accomplishing four years of consistent sobriety, and my mind is saying, "You can handle this, Cord, go ahead." Really?

The point is this. At that time, I was on a journey to sobriety. Four long years into my journey, but I was nowhere near actual sobriety. Long-term solid sobriety takes work. To recover fully from addiction and alcoholism takes work. Work that I had never done at that point.

At that time, I was white-knuckling every day to stay sober like so many others. Making it one day at a time. Going to a meeting every day, getting a sponsor, reading the Big Book, always working on my 4th Step, never sponsoring anyone because I hadn't been through the Steps. Praying and asking God to keep me sober "just for today," living my life in reservation about who I am because that's what they told me to do. It was a pathetic existence and one that was doomed to fail.

At that time, I hadn't been all the way through the 12 Steps, so I had no real sobriety. One little drink, and I was right back in the shit! Up to my eyeballs, and it was worse than it had ever been. One little drink and I spun completely out of control, losing everything I had gained over those four years. Waking up days later at a golf resort in Scottsdale, Arizona, not knowing how I even got there. Nine empty bottles of vodka scattered around the hotel room. I stayed out drinking for the next two years! Does this look like unmanageability to you?

There is an excellent description of "unmanageability" in "Step 2." The authors wrote about having trouble in relationships and lacking control over our emotional state of mind. How we can't make a living or have financial issues. That we are full of fear, feel useless, and are genuinely unhappy. That we have no connection to God or a higher power.

Answer these questions about your own manageability with a YES or NO:

- Am I currently having trouble with relationships?
  YES/NO

- Can I control my temper and emotions?
  YES/NO

- Do I feel useless?
  YES/NO

- Am I depressed, anxious, and miserable?
  YES/NO

- Do I have the job I really want?
  YES/NO

- Am I full of fear?
  YES/NO

- Am I unhappy?
  YES/NO

- Am I trying to connect with God daily by just asking him to keep me sober just today?
  YES/NO

- Am I any good to anyone else?
  YES/NO

The mental obsession that comes with alcoholism isn't just about your mind telling you it's okay to have a drink, as mine did in Las Vegas. It's not about sitting around all the time at home obsessing and thinking, "I just want a drink!" There are many different examples of mental obsessions in the Big Book. Like switching from hard alcohol to beer or wine. Deciding not to drink until after 5 p.m. Limiting the amount of alcohol you purchase and keep on hand. There's even the story about a man who put whiskey in milk to coat his stomach so he could drink more. Absurd behavior, wouldn't you agree?

Let's go back to my little Las Vegas faux pas. When I had that drink, did I have a normal or abnormal reaction to alcohol? Abnormal, of course! I experienced the phenomenon of craving. Once I had a drink, there was no sufficient reason great enough to keep me sober. It was game on! I couldn't control myself once I started to drink. I lost the power to choose once I took that first drink.

The most important thing to consider is fully conceding to your innermost self that you have no power. As long as you hold on to anything other than fully conceding to your innermost self that you are unmanageable and have no power, nothing else will work. It's a proven fact of the disease.

You will prove yourself wrong if you think that more knowledge, more meetings, a better sponsor, a better book, some new technology, or drugs will be enough to keep you sober. If you keep telling yourself, "I need more information, that's it, more information, that's the ticket. That will keep me sober." If you can't get this concept, there is no room for you to move on to Step 2. Because the next step tells us that we came to believe that there must be a power greater than us that will help us change our thinking. So if you are still hanging on to some other idea that anything else can keep you sober, there is no room to move on. And this is exactly what happened to me for several years. At that time, I bounced in and out of treatment centers, programs, and AA. In between sponsors and groups, looking for more information. Refusing to concede to my innermost self that my life had become unmanageable. That I had lost all control. That I had no power. That I couldn't stop drinking once I started. I was totally convinced of this. My actions during this time are proof of this. That without power, I am going to drink no matter what.

This is why the only thing that works is to fully concede, "I have no power to stop." To continue with daily prayer and meditation. To take time for daily reviews and work the 12 Steps. For me, working in addiction services at my treatment center and working with others is the only thing that will keep me sober.

To finish, Step 1, you need to answer these all-important questions YES or NO:

- Am I willing to concede to my innermost self that I am an alcoholic or addict?
  YES/NO

- Am I willing to concede that I don't have the power to quit once I start?
  YES/NO

- That my life is unmanageable because of it?
  YES/NO

My hope for you is that you will have a 1st Step experience.

What I mean by this is that right now, you are probably not feeling that good about yourself. You may feel like you are unmanageable and out of control. That you have no power and that you will keep drinking no matter what. You may be feeling a little queasy in the stomach, feeling a little despair, fear, and anxiety.

I'll let you off the hook for a minute and give you some hope. But first, I want to take the opportunity to tell you my 1st Step experience in the hope that it will give you an idea of what you are looking for and what you might experience on your own. Now, I don't want this to come off as Cord's drunk-a-log, but you need to understand first the extent of the circumstances to understand the outcome of my experience.

REACHING FOR THE BOTTOM

At the height of my drinking career, my life was so unmanageable, and out of control that looking back on it, you might think I made it up or that it wasn't possible. I was such a train wreck.

See, I was always the guy in control. I had money, a nice big home, new cars and was respected by all who worked for me and with me. I don't remember exactly when it all spiraled so out of control, but I can tell you that when it did, it was like watching a 747 come out of the sky in a ball of flames, and nothing could stop it.

How does one go from multi-millionaire by today's standards to dead broke and homeless? Addiction, depression and mental health issues, that's how. Just like me, left untreated, eventually It will strip you of everything you own and everyone close to you. No one is immune to the destruction of addiction.

My drinking issues went on for over 20 years, but at this point, within a year, everything came unwound on me. My wife left and took our daughter with her because of my drinking and financial troubles, which were due to my drinking. My business associates disowned me, and my business crumbled and burned to the ground until I was bankrupt.

I remember the day my wife left, and I found myself alone. I sat on the couch, staring at the television for the longest time and drinking. I don't believe I had ever felt that kind of misery, despair, and loneliness before. The more I drank, the more acceptable my current situation became.

Soon they came and turned off the power. I thought I don't really need power, do I? I had a bottle of alcohol. This is acceptable. Then they came and turned off the water, and I thought, I don't really need water, do I? I can shower at the community center when I really need it. Then they came and changed the locks on the front doors and removed me from my house, locking inside it, every single possession I owned.

I thought I don't really need a home, do I? I've still got a car. I can sleep there or find a cheap hotel. I have my alcohol, so this should be acceptable. I can make it work somehow. As long as I had my alcohol, it wasn't going to be that bad. In the depths of my addiction, each new low became okay as long as I had my drugs and alcohol. To me, it all became delusional and acceptable.

I moved to a small condo until I lost that. Then I lost my car to repossession. I borrowed a truck from a friend. I moved to a cheap hotel room that was close to the liquor store. I knew everything would work out. "I have enough money for alcohol so I can manage this," I thought.

What I thought was going to be a month or so, turned into a year. I walked to and from the liquor store every day to get what I needed. Borrowing, panhandling, and making it through one day at a time, not eating, and drinking to oblivion. During that year, I thought that I was starting to experience what might the bottom. I wasn't even close.

A year later, I found myself with back-to-back DUI arrests, one of which involved wrecking my friend's truck. He, of course, took it back from me. I found myself homeless. No car, no home, no money, on the streets of Salt Lake City. Living in a crappy hotel room or anywhere else, I could sleep and drinking 24/7. My children had written me off for dead. They believed that I had a death wish and was going to drink until I died. Many days, I wondered, "Have I found the bottom?" But I wasn't even close.

Over the next year, I survived on alcohol and nothing else and don't remember much about it. My days ran together and were spent from sun up to sun down in fear and anxiety about where I was going to find enough money for a bottle and to pay for the hotel room. I wasn't afraid of my own death or that no one in the world wanted anything to do with me. My fear was not having enough money to buy enough alcohol to last me through the day and night.

My daily regimen consisted of at least one-fifth (750ml) of vodka in the morning and then another one at night to get me to sleep before waking up, usually at about 3 a.m. to drink what was left so I could go back to sleep and then start all over again the next day. I would walk for miles from one liquor store to another each day, so the store clerks wouldn't notice how drunk I was and not sell to me. It was a routine that I started after a liquor store manager refused to sell to me one day because I was too intoxicated. I thought I had finally found my bottom. Not even close.

To finance my daily consumption of alcohol and the $19 I needed for the roach-infested hotel room, I had to go to extremes. For much of the next year, I found myself panhandling on the street corner near my hotel. Holding a sign that read, "Please

Help! VETERAN Needs Your Help!" scribbled in black marker on a piece of cardboard. I grew out my beard and wore a hat and dirty clothes so as not to be recognized.

I remember the horror I felt one day when a past business associate, his wife, and children stopped, rolled the window down, and handed me $5. I thought for sure they must have recognized me and then quickly surmised they hadn't. I thought my disguise must be pretty good. I didn't put the two and two together in my delusional state of mind, that I was down from my usual 190lbs to about 140lbs, dirty, unshaven, and was wearing some pretty ragged clothing.

During this time, I found that I could get just enough for the hotel room plus an additional $9.85 by begging for it. The extra was just what I needed for a fifth-size bottle of the cheapest vodka money could buy, and then I would walk to the liquor store to get my fix. Then usually would repeat this cycle if I ran out and needed more alcohol during the day. Often, I would think to myself, this must be the lowest place I have ever found myself. This has to be the bottom. Not even close.

I became angry. Angry at the world. Angry with God, and with myself. I felt like I was backed into a corner. I felt desperate but was determined that I wouldn't ask anyone for help, no matter what. I was convinced that no one cared anyway.

One night I had a new experience in my drinking. I had a violent withdrawal from alcohol and became extremely ill. So violently ill that I thought I was dying. I called my mother, a retired nurse, to tell her what was happening. She told me I needed to be hospitalized. That a catastrophic withdrawal from alcohol like this could cause a seizure, stroke, or heart attack.

Instead, I decided to drink more to try to compensate and stop the withdrawal while we talked. I drank an entire bottle of vodka in an attempt to feel better and passed out on the floor. I was trying to talk to my mother on the phone when it happened. I had a violent seizure while she listened. She called 911.

I woke to the sounds of emergency room personnel, doctors, and nurses. All rushing around doing what they were trained to do. A doctor was explaining to me that my heart had stopped, and they used paddles on me. A crisis worker came and asked me if I felt suicidal, and I said, "Are you kidding me? I certainly do! Can't you people just tell me how I get this over with? Must be the bottom? Not even close.

I was taken to the mental ward at the hospital for a nine-day detox. During my fabulous stay at Club Med, I had a visit from a doctor on call. He came in and in a very matter of fact way explained the current state of affairs. He said, "Mr. Beatty? You have alcoholic hepatitis and cirrhosis of your liver." I didn't know what that meant, so he told me, "Your liver has completely failed. An ultrasound shows no function. We need to do a biopsy."

That test showed the worst. My liver was shot entirely, and I was told there was no liver transplant available for people like me. He went on to tell me that I suffered from esophagitis and was bleeding internally. That my kidneys were failing as well, and my heart palpitations were the early signs of a stroke or heart failure.

I said, "What do we do to fix this?"

He said, "There is no fix, Cord. You have really done it this time. There is no liver transplant to be had and no recovery to be done." He told me to put my affairs in order, call my children and family, and that the hospital would do what they could to help make me more comfortable.

I asked him, "What am I supposed to do with this information now?"

He said, "Pray," and then left the room.

Found the bottom.

WHAT'S AT THE BOTTOM?

For the first time in my life, I realized what I had really done. That I had a real problem on my hands because of my drinking. During those days in the hospital, I experienced a tremendous amount of pain. I became very angry and withdrawn. I couldn't call my children or my family. I was heartbroken for what I had done to them. I was defeated, broken, and wanted to die. I couldn't face them after all of this.

About two nights into this, I couldn't sleep from the pain and the medication wasn't doing enough to really help, I had a visitor to my room.

Now, I have always thought that I may have been dreaming or delusional, but none-the-less, it seemed real. My visitor was tall, good looking, and a smooth talker. Neatly dressed, physically fit, and dripping with charisma. He sat in the corner of the room and started asking me questions. Uncomfortable questions about what my proposed immortality looked like and how he had an easier solution in mind.

The longer the questions and conversation went on, the more and more I became aware that this individual wasn't what I was expecting. He started telling me I had no one to turn to. He said he was the only one left who loved me. He had all the answers and everything I wanted here. I became extremely uncomfortable with him and the conversation and told him to leave. "Okay, I'll be around," he said.

What I did next actually surprised me. I rolled off the bed and fell to my knees, and I prayed. I prayed with more outward emotion than I have ever experienced. I had never done this before. I grieved for my children and begged for forgiveness for what I had done to them. Pleaded for God to take me off this earth. "Help me! Please, help me!" I cried!

I was at the bottom. I surrendered.

I was defeated, alone, and desperate. I was in so much physical and mental pain that I felt I couldn't take any more. I had the desperation of a dying man and pleaded with God, "I give up. Please, God, take me from this earth! I don't care, and I can't do this anymore. I don't know what you want of me. Please just take me now!" I cried myself to sleep.

And the next morning, as I described in the Prologue, I awoke to find myself staring at a bluebird through the window. All the pain, anger, depression, anxiety, and fear were gone. I had finally surrendered to God. I had finally figured out what powerless really meant. I didn't have God in my life and that he is what I needed. He had all the power, and I had none. I was powerless.

Four days later, and against medical advice, I walked out of the hospital. I called my mother and asked her if I could come home and stay for a while—I needed a safe place to disappear.

From the moment I awoke that morning in the hospital, I felt God's presence all around me. I was at peace and felt serenity like I had never experienced. It was as if I had angels surrounding me, keeping me safe, and watching over me. I knew that in this instance, God was doing for me what I couldn't do for myself. It was there. I finally had my 1st Step experience and began my journey to sobriety.

FINDING HOPE

I hope this gives you encouragement and hope. But let me give you some more before we begin Step 2. The authors of the Big Book wrote, "as soon as I can admit the possibility of God or of a higher power, I will be surrounded by a new feeling of power and direction that I have never experienced before as long as I am willing to take other needed steps." What it is referring to is finishing the other 11 steps.

When you read that, you will notice that the authors use the word "NEW." Not something from the past or an experience that you have already had. It talks about a new experience that you are ready to have and receive. This means a new direction for you. It means you are going to discover a new power like you have never experienced it before. And you are going to have a direction that you have never had before. This is what we have to look forward to.

Before finishing the 1st Step, I want you to explore what the word "powerless means again.

Ask yourself: *If I had the power to stop using and drinking, wouldn't I have already done this?*

So many people come to my treatment center in denial that a power greater then themselves exists. Many people come believing there is no God. I usually get this out of the way fairly quickly.

Let me ask you a question: How many times in your life have you been curled up on your bed in pain, misery, despair, and desperation? Broken, defeated, and hopeless? How often have you found yourself holding your hands and fists up to your face saying, "Please help me?"

My question to you is, "Who are you talking to?"

Ask yourself: *Is my life manageable, or has it become a three-ring shit show of chaos and confusion we talked about earlier?*

Ask yourself: *Can I fully concede to my inner most self, that I lack the power to fix my problems on my own?*

Congratulations on completing Step 1.

IF YOU GO
ALL THE WAY
THROUGH THE STEPS,
DO THE WORK
AS SUGGESTED,
AND THEN DECIDE
YOU ARE BETTER
OFF DRINKING
AND USING,
I WILL GLADLY
REFUND YOUR MISERY.

CHAPTER 2

SANITY

But seek ye first the kingdom of God, and his righteousness;
and all these things shall be added unto you.

—MATTHEW 6:33

I remember doing Step 2 for the first time. I thought for sure it meant I was going to be immediately well again. Returned to sanity. That I could stop drinking as soon as I finished up the 2nd Step and never pick up again.

Let's look at what it means to complete Step 2: "Came to believe that a power greater than ourselves could restore us to sanity." Notice the use of the word "could" restore you to sanity. To give you a really good idea of what you are going to be going through in this Step, let's discuss what it means to be at Step 10 for a minute:

- Done an inventory of your character defects (Step 4).
- Taken the exact nature of your wrongdoings to God and any other human beings (Step 5).
- Asked God to remove your character defects (Steps 6 and 7).
- Made a list of people you have harmed and made amends to all of them (Steps 8 and 9).

Assuming you have done all of this, you would experience the promise of Step 10: "I will have ceased fighting anything and everything—even alcohol. My sanity and thinking will be restored."

The point to realize here is just because you choose a power greater than yourself, doesn't mean that you will be cured of alcoholism. It doesn't mean your sanity will be returned either. You have to do a lot of work to get to that point.

BEING CLEAR ON STEP 1

In the Big Book, you'll notice Chapter 4, "We Agnostics," is entirely devoted to Step 2. In the first paragraph, the authors write about being clear about the distinction between being an alcoholic and a non-alcoholic. So, while you may not be clear on what is a real alcoholic yet, are you clear about what a non-alcoholic truly is?

If not, I would suggest you go back to the previous chapter and read about the differences between moderate drinkers, heavy drinkers, and real alcoholics. In *Alcoholics Anonymous*, the authors make the bold statement that if you are an alcoholic, you may be suffering from an illness that only a spiritual awakening can cure. I love this. Only one cure!

We are getting very clear at this point that if you are a real alcoholic, then the only solution is to a spiritual one. Nothing else will work. Let's turn this into a question.

Ask yourself: *If I am, in fact suffering from an illness that only a spiritual experience or intervention can cure, am I willing to consider this as a possibility or solution?*

Now, going back to Step 1:

Ask yourself: *Do I have the power to manage or conquer my alcoholism? Do I have the power to just not drink?*

In Step 1, you decided you can't do this. If I am a real alcoholic then, by conceding to my innermost self that I have no power, my only choice is to seek a power greater than me.

Okay. Assuming that you have experienced Step 1, let's move onto Step 2. If you haven't had a 1st Step experience, then why seek out a power greater than you to turn to? You should stop here and spend more time on Step 1 until you have an experience of your own.

If, however, you are hanging on to the idea that you have some choices left in your life. That maybe you still believe you can simply choose to not drink or use drugs. If you can do this, then you don't need the 12 Steps. Why go to meetings? Why get a sponsor? Why pray? Why work the steps? If you believe that you have the power to simply choose, then why haven't you exercised this power? Why are you still suffering? Ask yourself these questions and be honest with yourself.

I remember telling one of my sponsors that I had quit lots of times and how I could quit anytime I wanted to. He said, "If you can, then just stop! Why would you need me? But if you start again, then that's not quitting. That's not real sobriety. That's just taking a break from your misery."

FINDING POWER

We read that a lack of power is our dilemma. That we have to find a power greater than ourselves to live. But where do you find this power? Take a few minutes to consider the next question.

Ask yourself: *Where and how am I going to find power?*

The main objective of the 12 Steps is to show you how to find a power greater than yourself that can help you with your problems. To find a power greater than yourself to help you conquer your addictions. So if your main objective is to find a power greater than ourselves that will solve your problem, what is your problem?

It is your thinking!

My problem is my thinking. My solution is my drinking or using. Alcohol became a problem at some point, but up to then, it was a solution. So my main problem is not my drinking. It's my thinking. The 12 Steps can help me find a power greater than myself that will help me with my thinking. What we are talking about is finding a God of our understanding. Have you ever heard about this? A God of your understanding? So please consider the following statement for a moment:

> *The purpose of the 12 Steps is to find a God of my understanding. A power greater than myself that will help me conquer my life problems and addictions.*

YOUR IDEA OF GOD

Okay, let's now explore where and how to find this power.

Every man, woman, and child has a fundamental idea of God or higher power. We are born with it. Our fundamental belief may be clouded by ideas of church-going or worship or life issues, but in some form, it is there in all of us. That faith and proof of this power are older than humanity itself.

I think the first time I read this, I thought it was some of the most beautiful words I had ever read because I understood for the first time that the power of God, I was seeking was something I already had. It wasn't out there on a cloud somewhere as I'd always thought. I had always envisioned God being someone in the stars. A faraway place that I could never be close to. Reading these words helped me to understand that everything I was seeking was already inside of me. I was amazed. This work had my complete attention. I read that faith in some form of a higher power, or God is a part of our make-up. Like the feeling of having a close friend. That we sometimes have to search for this power, but it is always there with us.

This became so clear to me. Where am I going to find it? Inside myself. How am I going to find it? By searching myself fearlessly. What the authors mean by this is just to try it on for size. To have the courage to just try it. Consider this: If there is no fear involved, then there is no need for courage.

The idea of this is to search for a God of your understanding who you can find within yourself. To just try this or consider it as a possibility.

How many of you are afraid of walking through the 12 Steps at this point? Do you have a fear of sobriety, change, direction, or failure? Fear that this may not work for you. This is completely normal and should be embraced, not feared. I was too. But I went ahead and went through the 12 Steps. Why? Because I was willing to search fearlessly. I was willing to try.

I read about the issue of willingness in the Big Book and how as soon as I can show a willingness to believe that a higher power exists, I will see results. Even though it is impossible to comprehend God's power.

Think about this. Up to this point, all we really have done in Step 1 is to concede to our innermost selves that we have no power to create a spiritual experience on our own without a power greater than ourselves. All we have done in Step 2 so far is to become willing to try.

Ask yourself: *Am I willing to believe in something more powerful than me?*

Now stop and consider this statement:

> **For any of us to understand God, we would have to be God. Will we ever fully understand God?**

Humanity has tried, that's for sure. Wars have been waged, and blood shed, since the beginning of time because of humanity's selfish interpretations of God. This isn't about someone else's interpretation of what or who God is. It's about you finding a God of your own personal understanding. Whatever that may be.

Another thing that I realized in my sobriety was that we can't get closer to God than we already are and have been all our lives. I came to understand that the fundamental idea of God was deep inside me. How can we get any closer to God than that? As a result of going through the steps and doing the work, we may develop a better relationship with a God of our understanding. But we can't get any closer than we already are.

You don't need to consider anyone else's conception of God, because your own conception is sufficient enough to make a connection with God. When you admit the possibility that God exists, you will find that you experience a new sense of power.

By working through the 12 Steps, are you going to be driven by a new sense of power? A "new" sense of power meaning power like you have never experienced before in your life? Provided you take other simple steps along the way, taking Step 2 into your heart and mind will mean taking a direction you have never experienced before.

YOUR CONCEPT OF GOD

The authors wrote about our concept of God, not someone else's. What is important here is that it makes sense to you. A God of your understanding doesn't have to make sense to anyone but you. It doesn't have to make sense to your friends, sponsor, wife, relatives, or anyone else. Only to you. You might call this God by a different name, perhaps Source or Universe or Goddess or It.

Someone asked me once about my concept of God. I said, "He is tall, older, with long white flowing hair and beard, muscular in physique, carries a staff in his right hand, and is standing on a rock. He's a powerful-looking man. The wind is flowing through his long white robe and hair. He looks a lot like Charlton Heston in the *10 Commandments* movie to me." I added, "If you need to borrow him, I'll lend him to you for a while until you find your own concept of God." This is the concept of a God of my understanding that I share in this book, but please feel free to change name and gender to a God or higher power of your understanding.

A power greater than you could be anything that you choose it to be. It is important to understand that it also means a power you can't alter. You might consider that it means something non-human? I have heard of all kinds of descriptions of a power greater than me—everything from my wife, girlfriend, my car, my motorcycle, fly fishing, and my dog. Imagine trying to work an object like a dog into the 12 Steps. I have never really understood this logic because it talks about something non-human. Let's try it and see how it works. Let's put this into the steps:

> **Step 2:** Came to believe that my dog, Scooter, could restore me to sanity.
>
> **Step 3:** Made a decision to turn my will and my life over to Scooter as I understand him.
>
> **Step 5:** Admitted to Scooter, to myself, and to another human being the exact nature of my wrongs.
>
> **Step 6:** Were entirely ready to have Scooter remove all my defects of character.
>
> **Step 7:** I humbly asked Scooter to remove my shortcomings.
>
> **Step 11:** Sought through prayer and meditation to improve our conscious contact with Scooter as I understand him, praying only for knowledge of his or her will for me and the power to carry it out.

Does this make sense?

The point is to make sure you find a power greater than you. A non-human power is what you're seeking. Unless you believe that something human-made has the power to cure your afflictions? If you do believe that, then this process can't help you. All we are being asked here is to believe in a power greater than us. In other words, a God of your understanding.

Remembering what you've experienced in Step 1—that there was very little hope unless you had a complete physic change and no human power could produce it. Which means that you need to find power. Real power greater than yourself.

Ask yourself: *Do I believe, or am I willing to believe that there is a power greater than myself?*

If you can do that, then you are heading in the right direction. Being willing to believe in a power greater than us is the cornerstone of a spiritual foundation to build on. I learned early on when I was working in construction for my uncle that when a mason is building an archway, the very first brick laid is called the "cornerstone," and it determines the ultimate outcome of the strength and shape of the archway. Our cornerstone in sobriety is simply willing to believe in a power greater than ourselves.

A POWER GREATER THAN ME

I absolutely love this next part of our step work because it puts the greatness of our Creator into perspective. The absoluteness of a power greater than me. A God of our understanding who is omnipotent.

We read more information about relying on a higher power where the authors write that at some point in our drinking careers, we became alcoholics. With this came a crisis that we couldn't escape any longer. Because of this, we had to face the fact that God is all power and everything, or He is nothing at all. If He is all power and He is everything, then what is our choice going to be? To seek His power or go on the bitter end? Once again, pause to ask a couple of questions.

Ask yourself: *Did I become an alcoholic? Was I crushed by a self-imposed crisis that I couldn't postpone or evade? Did I do this to myself?*

The authors are asking us to consider a further question, so stay in this contemplative place:

Ask yourself: *Am I willing to consider that God is either everything with the power to take this from me? Or is he nothing at all? What is my choice?*

To finish, Step 2, you need to answer these all-important questions YES or NO:

- Do I believe, or am I willing to consider that there is a power greater than myself?
  YES/NO

- If there is a power greater than me, then what is my choice going to be? Is God everything, or nothing at all?
  YES/NO

- Am I going to continue to the bitter end, or am I willing to seek a power greater than myself to help solve my problem?
  YES/NO

If you have answered YES to these questions honestly, then congratulations, you are ready to move on to Step 3.

AM I WILLING
TO CONSIDER
THAT GODIS EITHER
EVERYTHING
WITH THE POWER
TO TAKE THIS
FROM ME?
OR IS HE
NOTHING AT ALL?
WHAT IS MY CHOICE?

CHAPTER 3

TURN IT OVER TO THE CREATOR

For I know the plans I have for you declares the Lord, plans to prosper you and not to harm you, plans to give you hope and a future.

—JEREMIAH 29:11

Finding a spiritual awakening is, in my opinion, the only true path to long-term sobriety. When I was in the military, I used to hear this a lot: "There are no atheists in a fox hole, boys." This is a true statement. If you were pinned down in a foxhole, the enemy had overrun your position. Death was imminent, and there was no way out, who are you going to reach out to?

Spirituality plays a vital role in sobriety. I grew up in an LDS family—that's the Mormons if you don't know. It gave me a strong grasp of the concept of God. I'm not much of a religious man, put on my Sunday best, go to meeting kind of guy, but I am a very spiritual person. However, I always find comfort and peace whenever I attend church meetings of any religion. Through the course of my journey to sobriety, I found a relationship with God that works for me.

I don't necessarily need to be in a church to be able to communicate with my Creator. I personally don't believe that church is the only place you can find God either. I do believe that we should have a connection with God outside of any place of worship, but everyone is different. Some people like to go to church, and some people don't. Some live by religious beliefs, and some don't. The point is to do what comes naturally and works best for you.

In the depths of my addiction, I stood in the doorway of death. I was in so much misery, pain, depression, and anxiety that only hell could compare, I suppose. Like being pinned down in a foxhole with no way out. Nowhere to run. No one to turn to except the one who created me. Fully conceding that I had no power to change my present situation. That no church could be my answer, but reaching for God would.

I believe that anyone who suffers from addiction will find sobriety sooner or later. Those of us who turn to God or higher power in these times in our lives will overcome addiction and be free for the rest of our lives. Those that don't are more likely to find sobriety in jail or in death. Either way, sooner or later, every alcoholic or addict finds sobriety one way or another.

Ask yourself: *Do I want to do this the easy way or the hard way?*

THE EASY WAY

I've tried it both ways, and here's what my experience is with that: Anyone who tells you that jail was a good experience or was no big deal is either lying or telling you this for a good reason. Speaking from my own experience, I can tell you that being incarcerated will strip you of any shred of dignity, pride, self-worth, self-confidence, and humanity that you ever had. No matter what I thought or had been told, once there, I was nothing less or more than every other loser in there with me. I can't think of anywhere on earth that is a more pathetic place to be. Truly hell on earth.

Now, in my opinion, there is an exception to this for a few people. There are those individuals who find sobriety when they are incarcerated. They find a higher power or God in that place. For these people, jail is the only place that will stop them from the devastation of the disease of addiction. This is one of the reasons I volunteer to teach a 12 Steps meeting at a jail near me. I do so in the hope of reaching any one of these individuals I am talking about.

Experiencing such a hellhole didn't keep me from drinking again. No amount of jail time made any difference to my thinking—even being behind bars. I knew that once I picked up, bad things would happen. There would be another DUI. Another court date. Another judge to see and eminently another stint of incarceration. Yet I did it anyway. Over and over. That's the insanity of this disease.

Nothing was bad enough to deter my addiction and behavior until I experienced standing at death's door. That was the only place that allowed me to realize that I only had one person left to ask for help. Only one place to go if I wanted to stay alive. Turns out, it was the easiest path of less resistance right in front of me all the time, and I couldn't see it.

I once had a sponsor who proclaimed himself an atheist. He

told me that I didn't need the 12 Steps or God to be sober. He said that all I needed to do is call him every day for instruction, rely on his every word, and attend meetings with him, and I would stay sober. What a load of crap! Of all the people I've met in AA, this guy was the worst. He was mean, ornery, and miserable.

Before long, I felt quite a lot of resentment toward this man and told him I didn't want him to be my sponsor any longer. Years later, I found myself still harboring the same feelings toward the guy. At the time, I had a mentor who was a religious leader and published author of many books on spirituality and recovery. He told me to let go of the resentment toward this man. Because he was an atheist, he had no fundamental belief in God or higher power. Therefore he was still suffering. He said, "Cord. Let it go. That man is not sober, he's just resting." Wow, did that make sense?

UNDERSTANDING YOUR PERSONALITY TYPE

Let's discuss personality for just a moment before moving on. Personality plays a huge role in turning our will over to God. I am talking about two different personality traits: Type A and Type B. This understanding is important because spiritual awakening isn't all that is needed to find sobriety. A physic change is needed, too. You have to change the way you have always thought and acted. The person you have been all the years in your addiction needs to die, and a new person needs to be born.

Working with people over the years with the 12 Steps, I have found that people with Type A personality traits tend to find it a little more difficult to turn their will over to God or their higher power. This is because Type A personalities are defined as a temperament characterized as excessive ambition, aggression, rigidness, competitiveness, drive, impatient, need for control, focused on quantity over quality, and unrealistic sense of urgency.

By contrast, Type B personalities are defined as living with less stress, more easy-going, non-combative, patient, and worry less.

I had a business partner who would argue with me about everything. It didn't matter what I brought to him; he would suddenly have a problem with it. He was negative, combative, opinionated, and rigid about everything. All of which is the reason I used the words "former business partner." So if you are a Type B, you are likely to find it hard to be around A Types for very long periods.

To gain more self-understanding about your personality, take a sheet of paper and write down the answers to these questions:

- Am I rigid?
- Am I easygoing?
- Am I combative?
- Am I hard to get along with?
- Am I impatient?
- Do I worry about everything?
- Am I positive or negative?
- Is there a single day in my life where I don't have conflict, anger, resentment, or worry?

If God is all power and love. Would you think then that God is a positive being? Someone impatient, worrisome, combative, or negative? Did he create the universe and everything in it by having this A-Type personality? No, just the opposite. God is a loving, kind, patient, easy-going, and positive. So if you are going to turn your will over to God, you may want to look at some of the things about the way you think first. If you are going to attempt to turn your will over to God with an expectation that it won't work for you, then that will most likely be your result.

TURNING YOUR WILL
OVER TO GOD

To complete Step 3, you need to have "Made a decision to turn your will and your life over to the care of God as you understand Him [Her or It]." But what does that mean to turn your will over? Does it mean no longer having freedom of choice? I don't believe that is possible. We are born with it. We established that we have no power in Step 1. However, we do have freedom of choice.

Think about this concept. Every living thing on this earth. Every animal, fish, bird, plant, or insect lives and exists obeying the laws of the will of God. Except for Man. Why? Because God gives us freedom of choice. Our issue is, how do we use it? In our case, it's our thinking. Our thinking is flawed, and we don't have the power to change it on our own. This is the reason we are where we are. So if that is the case, then we agree that we need to try something different.

The authors wrote that rarely has anyone failed by following in their path. What they are saying is that individuals who don't recover from alcoholism can't give themselves to a simple proven plan of action. In this case, the 12 Steps. They went on to say that people who fail are those who can't be honest. They are born this way, and never develop a way of being honest. They wrote that their chances of a successful outcome are very poor. They may even be suffering from a mental disorder. However, they may actually recover if they can change the way they have been living and become honest with themselves.

Look how clear this is? The authors tell us that if we want to have what they have, then we must follow in their path. Do what they do. They are telling us why we can't become sober? Why we can't be happy joyous and free from alcohol? Because we won't give ourselves completely to this program and to a higher power. Something or someone greater than ourselves.

Ask yourself: *Am I willing to ask God to take away the compulsion to use alcohol and drugs from me for good? Not just for today, but for good? Am I willing to stop drinking and using for good? Do I have a desire to stop for good?*

Everyone who honestly goes through the 12 Steps has the same experience that Bill W. had. The same experience as my sponsors and members of AA and the same experience me. As a result of going through the Steps, I had a spiritual experience. A "spiritual awakening." The compulsion to drink or use drugs was removed from me, and I was separated from my addiction. As a result of this, I experienced a new power. One I had never had before. I felt as if God had made a deal with me.

I felt as if God had said, "Cord, you will never have to drink or use drugs again. You will never have to suffer the way you have for so long. All I am going to ask of you is that you have faith in me, allow me to steer your ship for you. All I ask is that you take this message of hope and a simple proven plan of action to others who still suffer. Are you in?

I said, "I'm in!" That's a pretty easy gig, wouldn't you agree?

When this happened, as a result of going through the steps, I have to say that it sounded like a pretty good deal. And I can guarantee that if you go through the 12 Steps and follow the path, you will never have to suffer the way you have been again. You will never have to live the way you've been living again. It doesn't matter who you are. How new you are to sobriety or how long you've been sober. You don't have to live the way you've been living if you dedicate the time to the 12 Steps and Promises.

The authors teach us about having our "own experiences." They tell us that if we want what they have, and we are willing to go to any length as they were, then we are ready to take additional steps. They are talking about Steps 3 to 12.

Let's turn this into a couple of questions.

Ask yourself: *Do I want what they have? Have I made this decision? Am I willing to go to any length to get it? Am I willing to walk through the rest of the steps and have my own experiences?*

If the answer is YES, then you are ready to move forward.

GOD HAS ALL THE POWER

I had an experience years ago concerning these questions. I had some long-term sobriety under my belt and had opened my first alcohol and drug treatment center. I was sharing the message of hope and sponsorship with a few different men. I met a young man named Lance, who asked me to be his sponsor. Lance was in and out of sobriety, and I thought that maybe I could help him find his way through the 12 Steps.

At the time, Lance was 19 and had been an addict since he was about 10 or 11 years old. At some point, he had returned to Seattle to live with his mother. I had been his sponsor for about six months before he went home. Lance called me one day and told me he was in a lot of trouble, so I suggested he came to the treatment center. He agreed, and we made the arrangements with his parents.

Over the next six months, we became close friends as we worked through the 12 Steps. I watched this bright young man grow and learn. I listened to his future hopes and dreams. We fished, hiked, worked on fences, tended horses, and did chores all the while working on the 12 Steps. He became stronger with every passing day. We worked on mending the broken relationship with his parents. He began to call home more often and spend time talking to them. Letting them know he was doing great and that he loved them.

Lance wanted to attend college but needed to finish high school, get his GED, and needed a driver's license. I helped him with this and assisted him with his enrollment in college. I helped him get moved into an apartment so he could attend college and helped him through some of his fears and anxieties of starting college and moving on in his life.

Shortly after Lance moved, I received a call from someone living near his school. I learned that Lance had relapsed, overdosed on heroin, and died that night in his room. It was devastating. To make things worse, I had to call his parents and break the news to them.

Now, I don't have many words that can truly describe the experience of listening to a mother wail in grief and a father breakdown and sob from the news of losing a child to addiction. The only thing that was going through my mind at the time was that I was at fault. This happened on my watch. He was in my care. I thought that I was to blame for his death because there was no one else but me to point to. I had never felt this amount of guilt and shame.

Then I learned his parents would be traveling to see me to retrieve Lance's body for a funeral, and I would have to face them. A funeral that I would have to take part in. A ceremony where everyone would be talking about me or blaming me for his death because they had left Lance in my stewardship, and I had failed him.

These thoughts devastated and humiliated me. Broke me to my core. All I could think in the ensuing sleepless nights and miserable days following was that I could have done more. I made another phone call. I could have taken him to another meeting. He talked him out of college enrollment and kept him at the center longer. Maybe I could have worked more with him on the step work and his spiritual awakening. I was defeated, and I wanted to quit. To shut the doors of the treatment center and never sponsor anyone again. I wept for days, and my mind took me to the darkest places of my addiction. Thoughts of relapse and despair enveloped me. It took me to a place where I thought alcohol would be the only solution. I don't know that I had ever felt so alone in my misery.

I turned to a sponsor and mentor. We talked about what had happened and how it had affected me. He asked me if I was willing to go to any length to defend my sobriety. If I was willing to do anything for my sobriety and I said yes. He said, then you need to pray, and you need to do it right now! He said, "You need to ask God for the strength to take away the pain of this horrible situation to allow you to continue your journey. You need to pray that Lances' parents will be comforted and forgiving toward you. You have got to turn this over and surrender this to God with as much conviction as the day you asked God to remove the compulsion to drink from you."

And so I did. I got down on my hands and knees and surrendered. I prayed, "God? I can't shoulder this burden alone. It's more than I can bear. Father, please take this burden from me and let me continue in my sobriety. Free from my addictions. Please comfort Lance's parents, brother, and sisters. Please help them forgive me, Amen." I didn't feel any immediate relief and was very disappointed, but there is an old saying about how God works in mysterious ways. I always wondered what it really meant. I was about to find out.

A few days later, Lance's entire family came to Utah and drove to the treatment center to meet with my business partner and me. I was petrified to face the devastation and grieving they must be experiencing. I watched hopelessly as the whole family came through the front door. They all gathered around me, embraced me with loving open arms, and told me they loved me.

They told me how much they loved and appreciated me for giving them six months of continued conversations over the phone, photos, and news of Lance's growth. Six months they would have never had with Lance had it not been for my involvement in his life, and that of the others at our center. During those six months, they witnessed the same things I did. We all did. They watched him grow and become sober. They heard all about his hopes, dreams, and newfound happiness. They told me that the last time they had witnessed Lance so at peace and happy was when he was 11 years old before they had lost him to addiction. They thanked me for sharing my love and hope with their son.

We spent hours poring over photographs, belongings, and walking the property while they listened to me recite stories of Lance riding the four-wheelers, fishing the river with me, throwing a baseball back and forth, and taking care of the horses.

From my own experience, I can promise you this. If you are willing to surrender your heaviest burdens and your will to God, he will be there! He was everywhere around me during those days. His loving presence consumed me, my thoughts, my heart, and my soul. He was with me all the way through the funeral, where I was asked to speak about Lance and my experiences with him. God comforted his parents and me in ways I would have never been able to imagine.

From that day forward, I knew with conviction that I was doing exactly what I was supposed to be doing with my life. That I had to stay strong and to stay sober. You see, I wasn't the teacher in this situation. God had used Lance to teach me, and I was but a student. Through Lance, I had learned about loving another who was suffering, humility, kindness, patience, and the joy this brings. For the first time in my life, I learned just how much God loves us and is there for us when we need him the most.

Next time you are having difficulty in your life and sobriety, just stop . . .

Ask yourself: *Would I be willing to get on my knees right here and right now and ask God for help? Would I be willing to do anything he asks of me?*

BELIEVING IN SOMETHING BIGGER

At the beginning of Chapter 5 in *Alcoholics Anonymous*, the authors suggest that God has all the power we need, and we should seek him now! It doesn't say my name. It doesn't refer to anyone else. It only refers to God. It says the "One" who has all power. It doesn't say, "Cord, who has all the power." I don't have any power. He has all of the power. May we find him now!

The authors refer to the ABC's. We hear these recited in AA meetings. We read about them in Chapter 5 in the Big Book. We admit that at some point, we became alcoholics, and our lives have become unmanageable. We believe that no human power can take away our suffering and that God will if we seek him.

Let's turn all of this into a few questions.

Ask yourself: *Do I believe I am an alcoholic? Do I believe I can't manage my own life as it is today? Do I believe, or am I at least willing to believe in the idea that no human power can deliver me from alcoholism? Am I willing to believe that if I seek God, he could and would help me if I ask him?*

If you answer YES to these questions, then you should feel convinced of this. If that is the case, then you are in Step 3. You have decided to turn your will and life over to the care of God as you understand him. What does this mean? What do you do?

Ask yourself: *What does it mean being convinced? At this point, am I convinced that only God can relieve me of this misery if I seek him out?*

Next, the authors say that the first requirement is to admit the following:

When my life runs on self-will, it can't be a success.

The authors describe unmanageability and what a life run on self-will would look like. When I went through this part with my sponsor, I was asked to read this part of Chapter 5 in the Big Book in the first person. I was asked to use the words to develop my own experiences about my life. Not as if I was reading about someone else but about me. Take a few minutes to do the same exercise. Read through Chapter 5 in the first person. How does it compare with your life?

I found this experiment quite amazing, and the following is my own story derived from this exercise. It shows just how unmanageable my own life had become.

The first requirement in seeking a connection with God is that I will be convinced I have been living my life on self-will, and I have proven that this has not been successful. I have always been in a constant battle with somebody or something, no matter how hard I try.

I have been living my life through self-seeking and selfishness. I am like an actor who is trying to be a director and run the entire production on my own. If only the other actors did as I asked, my show would be amazing! Everyone would be pleased. Life would be wonderful!

To persuade everyone to do as I wish, I am kind, considerate, giving, patient, and self-sacrificing. What they don't really know about me is that deep down, I am mean spirited, egocentric, dishonest, and selfish. But hey? Isn't everyone?

So what usually happens? My production doesn't work out very well. People around me are disappointed again. I am convinced that life doesn't treat me very fair. So I decided to try harder, becoming more demanding, angry, and egotistical. Or, if need be, I become more kind and loving to get what I want.

Still, my show doesn't come off very well. I may have to admit that I may be somewhat at fault? But I am sure that everyone else is more to blame than me. I become resentful and self-pitying. So what then is my basic trouble? Even when I am trying to be virtuous and kind, I am really just a self-seeker.

Am I delusional? Do I believe that I can achieve happiness and satisfaction if only all of the rest of you would manage yourselves as I wished? Isn't it clear to you that this is what I want? Don't you know or understand who I am?

And yet, my actions make each, and every one of you retaliate against me, taking all that you can from my show. It is clearly evident that even in my best attempt as a director, I am nothing more than a producer of confusion instead of harmony.

I admit that I am selfish, self-centered, ego-centric, and dishonest. I am like the retired salesman lying in the Florida sunshine complaining about the sad state of our affairs. I am like a lawmaker who is sure all would be paradise if all of you would only behave yourselves. I am like a criminal who believes society has wronged me. I am the alcoholic and addict who lost everything and is locked up.

Whatever the case may be, I am really only concerned about myself, my selfish needs, resentments, and self-pity. The root of all of my problems is my selfishness, dishonesty, and self-centeredness! I'll step on the toes of anyone who gets in my way, knowing they will retaliate against me. Sometimes, they hurt me without warning. But consistently, it is because, in my past, I have made decisions based on my worst character defects that place me in a position to be hurt.

I recognize that my troubles are of my own making. They are who I am. I am a fine example of self-will run riot, though I usually don't think so. I know deep down inside that I must be rid myself of this dishonest and selfish conduct. I must or will die from it!

I know that God makes this possible. And I know that I can't find a way out without his help. I have had demonstrations of this all throughout my life, but couldn't change any of it, even though I wanted to. Nor could I rid me of my selfish, self-centeredness by trying on my own. I had to have God's help.

Through this exercise, I identified my problems, and they were of my own making. My self-centeredness and self-pity and self-seeking were my own. I've found that everyone in sobriety has troubles and issues. We all do. I found that by reading that part in the first person, I could identify with all of them. I felt like all of this was written about me. I have had every one of those issues at some point in my life. Give this a try yourself.

Again, let's turn this into a couple of questions.

Ask yourself: *Am I willing to consider that selfishness, self-seeking, and self-centeredness are the root of my troubles? Am I willing to consider that my troubles are of my own making?*

I put these to use in my own world, asking myself these questions and more. If I can concede that selfishness, self-seeking, and self-centeredness are the root of my troubles, then maybe I can start to deal with them instead of constantly calling up my sponsor or someone else to whine about poor ole me. Telling them about all my troubles and that everyone else in my life is at fault.

The authors are telling me that I am driven by a hundred forms of fear—self-delusion, self-seeking, and self-pity. If I am driven by self-delusion, then how would I ever know if I am delusional? I would not. If I am self-delusional, I will never know when I am actually delusional because I lack the power to know the difference. I don't have the power to overcome my current state of mind.

This is another really good reason to go through the 12 Steps and especially to go through them with a sponsor. Someone to hold us responsible because we are incapable of knowing if we are self-delusional because we lack power. Can you see what a trap this puts us in?

A HUNDRED FORMS OF FEAR

Let's talk about fear. Do you have a hundred forms of fear? Fear that these steps won't work? Are you willing to accept that they won't unless you find power? Real power. By doing the steps and living the principles, you will find that fear will begin to fade. That the steps will begin to work for you. I can promise you that it worked for me and it will work for you. Before I even got to the end of the 12 Steps, I had lost any compulsion to drink. My thinking and my attitude were completely different than when I started.

When I first started studying the 12 Steps and attending meetings, I didn't think I needed it or would be a part of it for very long. I treated it like a convenient place to stop off to satisfy a court order or two and keep everyone, including my family, off my back. I didn't want to work the Steps. I was in and out of sobriety and the program. But by the time I finally conceded that I needed help and got to the end of the Steps, my thinking had changed. I would call this "physic change." If I had known all along that it was going to be as great as it is to be sober, I would have started sooner. I would have done a little better job and stuck with the program from Step 1.

HOW TO STOP PLAYING GOD

Okay, back to our problem. We found the problem, now let's find the solution. It tells us the how and why of it. That we have to stop playing God and decide he is going to be our director. Admitting he is our father, and we, his children. The authors write that good ideas are simple ones and can lead us to freedom.

There is a couple of things to think about here. First, the authors wrote about a keystone of the new and triumphant arch for which we walk through. Remember the cornerstone from Step 2—the first brick that the mason lays? The keystone is the stone in the very middle top of the arch, which holds it together.

My cornerstone was my beginning. My willingness to believe in a power greater than me. The keystone which is holding it all together for me is that I need to stop playing God. Do you see how simple this solution is?

Ask yourself: *Do I have a solid partnership with God as I understand Him today? A true partnership means an equal position of power, do I have that with God? If God has all of the power, and He is everything, then how could that ever be a partnership?*

If you are working for someone else, are you in partnership with the owner or manager above you? Is your employer your partner or your boss? You do the work you're supposed to do. Your employer pays you and gives you what you need to do your job the way you are supposed to do it. Does this make sense?

So providing that we work on the solution or that we stop playing God and do his work, we will be guaranteed certain promises which we will find next in the 3rd Step promise. We read these promises in Step 3, in Chapter 5 of *Alcoholics Anonymous*.

The 3rd Step promise tells us that if we stop playing God, remarkable things will follow. We will have a new employer. He is powerful and provides all we need if we stay close to him and do his work. If we do this, we become less interested in ourselves and more interested in contributing to life. We will feel a new power and enjoy peace. We discover that we can face life with success. We become conscious of God's presence and begin to lose our fears. It clearly states that we are "reborn."

This is so amazing and powerful! God truly doesn't have favorites, but he pays his employees very well. This has also been my experience. So if I am willing to do what is suggested and let God be the director and I be his agent to do his will, then I will experience the promises that are outlined in Step 3, which read, "We were reborn." Meaning that the person who I have been for so long has to die for a new me to be born.

This has also been my experience. I have been told that I am not the same person that everyone knew when I was drinking. My children have told me they have never seen their father so happy, joyous, and free. That I am easier to get along with. That I am at peace with myself and my surroundings. I have to agree. Because earlier in my sobriety, I was reclusive. Not too friendly and didn't want to be in "your" program. I didn't want to talk to anyone or say the words, "I am alcoholic."

At one of my first AA meetings, I met an older man named Jim. "Gentleman Jim," everybody called him. They referred to him as one of the old-timers in AA. I was impressed by his years of sobriety. I loved hearing Jim share in meetings because I knew that everything that came out of his mouth, I could count on.

One day I approached Jim and asked him for some advice. I asked what he thought my chances of staying sober were. To my surprise, Jim snapped at me with a boom in his voice. His exact words were "Slim to f**king none!" Scared the hell out of me. It wasn't exactly what I had in mind for advice.

I remember it made me feel a little angry and resentful toward the program. It made me think maybe this wasn't for me. But you see, I was the guy that was still completely out of control, unmanageable, and still trying to run the show all by myself like I had it all figured out. Turns out, Jim was a pretty good judge of my character in those early days because it took me a lot longer than I thought to finally get it.

Here we are at Step 3, and we are being asked to make a decision.

Ask yourself: *Am I willing to make a decision to turn my will and my life over to a God of my understanding?*

What I was taught about this was that this is a two-part question. The first part is "my will." The real definition of a will is really a set of instructions. The second part of this is my life. I am making a decision to turn my life over to God to do with me as he wants. Not as I will.

Later, when we get to Step 12, we will learn what the real meaning of this is. The real work will begin at Step 12. The first 11 Steps will prepare us to do the real work.

Remember the deal I made with God when he told me I would never have to drink again if I did his will and his work? All he asks me to do is to take this message hope to others who still suffer. Pretty easy gig to keep my sobriety.

What I would like you to do is to take a few minutes or some time to consider what you are about to do. What you are about to ask for. It was my own experience that after I did this Step, it was different for me from then on. There was a change in my attitude and spirit. Because when I did this, I gave myself to God. I surrendered everything to him and asked him humbly to take this burden away from me.

Step 3 is a big one, and I can promise you that if done properly with the utmost conviction, sincerity, and humility, it will change your life forever!

FINDING EVERYTHING, YOU NEED

When you take this step, God will give you everything we need. So if you are willing, please find a quiet place and walk through this. Please take this time to kneel and pray. You can come up with whatever words work for you from this outline. Here is an example of the Step 3 prayer that I used for myself.

> God, I offer myself to you. To do with me as you will. I ask that you relieve me of the bondage of myself. The burdens I have created by living a life in self-will. Please take away my difficulties and grant me victory over them. Show me the way to live and share your power, your love, and your way of life with others. May I do your will always.
> Amen.

I gained a lot of momentum from this prayer when I did it with my sponsor. Mostly because he took the time to really explain to me this prayer and its promises, which I would like to share with you the way he did with me.

The first part of the prayer says, "I offer myself to God to do with me as you will." Meaning I am now committing to no longer be steering my own ship. That I turn over the controls and direction to God.

The next part reads, "Relieve me of the bondage of self" or "myself." It means my thinking. We are saying, "Help me, God, to change the way that I think so I can better do your will, not mine."

The next part says, "Please take away my difficulties" or my alcoholism, addiction, problems, or mental health issues. Please remove my desire and compulsion to drink so that I can share your message of hope with others. So that I can clearly tell them about your love, your power, your way of life. Please do this for me. Keep me sober, and I will do your will always.

If you have sincerely completed the 3rd Step prayer and committed yourself to receive its promises, then congratulations. You are now ready to move on to Step 4.

GOD TRULY
DOESN'T HAVE
FAVORITES,
BUT HE PAYS
HIS EMPLOYEES
VERY WELL.

CHAPTER 4

INTO ACTION!

The only impossible journey is the one you never begin!

—TONY ROBBINS

Moving into Step 4, Chapter 6 of *Alcoholics Anonymous*, I'd like to point out that in the previous chapter, the authors wrote that next, we launched into a vigorous course of action. A personal housecleaning, which we have never done before.

I love this! Notice it says; "we launched" not sat around and thought about the state of the union. It doesn't say we kind of meandered on out there after coffee and tea. It says loud and clear, we "LAUNCHED!"

A good example of my own experience of Step 4 came with some personal goals. When I finished the 12 Steps and found my peace, I set my sights on traveling to Nepal and Mount Everest.

I wanted to climb the Himalaya to show others that anything is possible in sobriety. After all, alcoholics and addicts are climbing mountains every single day. To accomplish this, I knew I needed to launch into a vigorous action if I wanted to achieve success. Physical training, hiking, walking, running, and a solid mental focus would be required for success.

I couldn't accomplish the goal by sauntering out every morning for a leisurely walk in the woods, followed by a heavy meal and a cigarette. I didn't just talk about it every day saying to myself and others, "Someday I'll get there. Someday I'll climb those mountains." No. I knew it would take physical and mental conditioning to do this.

I prayed for strength and then turned it all over to the man! Surrendered my will and the outcome to him. A year later, I was in Nepal, making my way high into the Himalayan mountains, climbing the ice, snow, and reaching for the unimaginable. Planting an ice ax in the snow inscribed with the words: *In Memory of "Lance" and those who still suffer.*

The authors wrote that they vigorously went after this next step to do their own personal housecleaning in the same manner. That next, we need to launch into a vigorous course of action. This decision is a vital step, which won't have a long-term effect unless followed by a tireless effort to get rid of the things that are blocking us. Alcohol is only a symptom, so we have to get to the bottom of the cause.

This is what you just experienced in Step 3. You should now be feeling more connected with God or your higher power. You should now have a feeling of confidence and power that you haven't experienced before. If you do and don't immediately move into Step 4, you will lose this connection, and the power will fade.

REMOVING BLOCKS

Your primary purpose in Step 4 is to uncover and deal with the things within you that are in the way or blocking you from a connection with a God of your understanding. If you can't see God, then you can't hear him either. If you can't communicate with God, or a higher power, because of the things within you that are keeping you from doing so, then you can't move forward.

This means getting down to causes and conditions. The definition of cause is a person or thing that gives rise to an action, phenomenon, or condition. The definition of the condition is the state of something, especially about its appearance, quality, or working order. In other words, your state of mind.

If this is true then you need to discover the exact state of mind, which is blocking you from direct communication with God. What I found was that if I am blocking myself from God, then I have absolutely no power to stay sober. I can't be happy joyous and free if I am blocking myself from seeing and communicating with God.

HOW FREE DO YOU WANT TO BE?

The authors write that they started a personal inventory in Step 4 and explain that a retail business that doesn't take an inventory won't work. This is a fact-finding and fact-facing process that takes effort but helps us discover the truth. They write that the process is meant to disclose unsalable goods and get rid of them without regret. This is what is needed if the business is going to have success.

Taking a personal inventory of the character defects within you that are blocking you from a connection with God, or your higher power, is what this is all about. It's a fact-finding mission. It's not supposed to be fun but very needed if you are to be sober. And this is what we must do with your life. The authors wrote that they took an inventory honestly, searching out flaws that caused their failures. Once they were convinced that it was their lives run on self-will that had defeated them, they were able to clearly see their character defects.

It won't do you much good to inventory the positive things about yourself because they aren't in the way of your connection with God. A good example that was given to me on this was to put this in an asset vs. liabilities view in the first person.

Ask yourself: *Do my assets and positive things about me cause any of my problems?*

My liabilities, on the other hand, are all to blame. My shortcomings and defects of character. That side of me is a complete troublemaker.

Years ago, I was attending an aftercare program as part of a sentence from a DUI I had gotten myself into. Mostly consisting of group therapy sessions—which I hated just for the record. During a 4th Step discussion, the counselor brought up this topic. She said we needed to take inventory of our assets along with our defects.

I thought, "Why? Have my assets and the good things about me caused me misery and failure? Are they the reason I drink, get drunk, drive my car when I could hurt someone? Are they the reason I was pulled over and arrested for driving drunk? Are they the reason I am here in this class? I hate so much right now. I think not!" My liabilities, however, are all to blame. These are the things that keep me from being sober. Keep me from a connection to God.

IDENTIFYING RESENTMENTS

Back to where we were. We identify resentments as our number-one offender. Alcoholics are destroyed by resentment. Resentment causes spiritual disease, mental and physical illness. The authors of the Big Book do a masterful job of identifying the spiritual malady of alcoholism. When spiritual sickness is overcome, their lives straightened out physically and mentally. They provide a way for us to do this. They tell us to set our resentments on paper and list them all: institutions, people, and others to whom we harbor resentments. They tell us we must look at why we are angry, what the cause is, how it makes us feel, and, ultimately, what our part is so we can deal with the issue.

The authors write that when we overcome our spiritual sickness, we can correct our mental and physical problems. This is correct, wouldn't you agree? Then it tells us how to take care of resentments. Because if we are to be free from alcoholism, and continue living, we have to be free of anger and resentments. Resentments and anger are luxuries for normal people. For the alcoholic, they are poison. The authors go on to provide an example of looking at our resentments in a different light. To see how they dominate and run our life; how they have the power to "kill" the alcoholic.

This doesn't necessarily mean that my resentments can kill me physically, but they can kill me spiritually. They can kill my hope, inspiration, happiness, motivation, etc. And in some cases, eventually, for the alcoholic or addict, resentments will kill them physically.

Have you ever heard someone say, "That guy's a dry drunk?" They are referring to this kind of person. Someone with a lot of resentments who attends meetings every day to stay sober but is an ornery, mean, self-centered, and selfish individual. He's the guy who usually says, "I'm grateful that I am sober just for today."

When I hear this in a meeting, I always think to myself, "Wow, just for today? Not the rest of your life?" This is the guy who is sober today and in meetings, but spiritually dying and eventually may die physically if he doesn't change his thinking.

It has been my personal experience when I attend AA meetings, I can only experience one of two things: I'm either hearing what I need to hear and getting worse, or I am getting better. You can have the same experience attending religious or spiritual meetings. If you attend a religious meeting, you are either getting stronger spiritually or getting weaker, depending on your mindset willingness to listen.

I've found that AA, in church, or spiritual meetings have found one thing in common: they are all very positive experiences because I go there with an open mind and heart. I am willing to accept and listen. I've never left anyone of these meetings, saying to myself, "Oh, did that suck!"

Ask yourself: *Do I want to get better, or do I want to get worse? How free from do I want to be?*

Let's walk through the example of taking a proper inventory. Take a piece of paper and make four columns. In the first column, write your resentments. In the second column, write the cause of the resentment. In the third column, write how it makes you feel. In the last column, you look at your part in the resentment. Where can you see your character defects—specifically see four of them:

- Selfishness
- Dishonesty
- Resentment
- Fear

Here is a good step by step example of how to write down and deal with resentment to see my character defects.

1. In the first column, I write: *"Mom kicked me out of the house."*
2. In the second column, I write: *"She kicked me out because of my drinking."*
3. In the third column, I write: *"It made me feel abandoned, hurt, unloved, and afraid."*
4. In the fourth column, I write: *"My part is my selfishness, dishonesty, fear, and resentments. I was selfish not to seek help to stop. I lied about using, stole Mom's jewelry, and money. I feared she wouldn't love me if she found out."*

Do you see how simple this exercise can be? Keep it simple and don't complicate the inventory and you will be through it in no time. As you write your inventory, try to disregard the other person's involvement entirely and focus more on your part. Your character defects in your part of the resentment. Where were you to blame? Your inventory belongs to you, not the other person you are listing. When we see where we are at fault, then we list them. We admit our wrongdoings honestly, and we become willing to make things right.

IT'S YOUR PROBLEM!

I always thought that character defects were other people's problems, not mine. Early on, I would go to meetings and people watch. I thought I was getting better by noticing everyone else's defects and none of my own. I was judgmental toward most people.

When my sponsor and I first worked through Step 4, we talked about this. He asked me if I thought I had any defects of character that I needed to discuss with him. I said, "I don't think so." He suggested that I go to the next meeting and note down what other people talked about so we could meet discuss my position on this again.

So I did. I thought this was a great exercise and would show my sponsor that I was the one guy in AA who had no defects of character. That I would prove to him once and for all that I was flawless. Perfect in every way. And so I did.

I went to the next meeting I could find. I was actually pretty excited about the challenge—like a little kid in a classroom. A look of determination on my face, pencil and paper in hand, tongue protruding slightly out of the corner of my mouth as I listened and wrote: "That guy over there he's selfish. That guy speaking is arrogant and dishonest. She's angry and delusional. He's sleazy. They are all dishonest, self-pitying, blaming everyone else, self-loathing! Slut! Asshole! My list could on ad infinitum in this place," I thought.

I was so excited to get back to see my sponsor and show him what I found out. I said, "Check this out. I made my list like you asked me to. Dude, these guys are sick! I mean, really sick!"

He read through my list and pushed it back across the table to me and said, "Well, there you have it. You just wrote down all of your character defects."

"What?" I said. "Now wait just a minute. I'm not dishonest, self-pitying, and selfish. I'm not an asshole, at least I think I'm not, and I am certainly not a slut!"

He said, "Didn't you just get through telling me how one of your biggest problems is telling people what they want to hear? That you were in this for yourself? That you really don't care about what everyone else is doing or if they get better? What matters to you is only that you get better?"

What I was discovering was that I was witnessing characteristics in others that I had been unwilling to see in myself. As we write our inventory, we review our fears, ego, sex problems, and continue to identify our greater character defects. Where we have been selfish, dishonest, and whom they had hurt. How we have created jealousies, suspicions, deceit, and resentments in our relationships.

There is a lot of worksheets out there that show you how to take your inventory. Most of them are all the same ideas but laid out differently. I still think the one given in the Big Book on page 65 is the best. Notice that it is dealing with resentments. To go over the instruction again. The first column lists which are resentment toward, the second column is what caused the resentment. The third column is how it made me feel. As a suggestion, you should write a fourth column that reflects your part and which of the four-character defects are present—fear, selfishness, dishonesty, resentments.

This is an example only. There are many ways to do your inventory, but it is a very simple process. There is no way to do it wrong. It will probably won't be the only time you do this either. And before you start, remember what the authors wrote:

If you have made a decision to do a searching fearless moral inventory and created a list of your character defects, you have a good beginning.

What this is saying is that at this point, you have made a decision (Step 3). You have made an inventory of your defects of character (Step 4), and you have made a new beginning (change). It doesn't say you're done. It would be impossible to cover every character defect you have in just one inventory list.

IT'S NOT A ONE-TIME THING

People who are constantly working on their inventory are happier. The more inventory and time that goes by, the more their character defects fade away. Let's identify an example of a character defect and a possible solution to help understand how to deal with this.

When I went through this the first time, my sponsor suggested that he write things down for me so that I could concentrate on what I needed to do and what I was about to go over with him. He said, "This way, we will do Steps 4 and 5 at the same time together." The authors wrote that it is best to discuss these things with another person once you're finished with the inventory. It means:

> *You may not overcome drinking if you don't complete an inventory and how learning about honesty, humility, and fears are best discussed with another person.*

This is the way Steps 4 and 5 were done in the 1940s. Why would we change it now? It worked for them, it worked for me, and it will work for you. It was meant to be done with someone else and in this way.

If you have been around AA for a while, it's important to have an open mind. What if you find someone who has less sobriety than you, but that has gone through all 12 Steps like this and had experienced a physic change and spiritual awakening? Grab ahold of them. The length of sobriety is not important. Knowledge and experience are. Wouldn't it make sense to listen and learn from them? It doesn't matter if you are new or if you have been through the steps multiple times.

If you keep an open mind as you go through the 12 Steps this way, you will have a few things happen. You will have a new experience with the Steps that you haven't had before. And you will discover things about yourself that you didn't know. When I was having difficulty with this, my sponsor always asked me, "How free do you want to be?

Ask yourself: *How free do I want to be?*

In the example I gave earlier about "my mother kicking me out of the house," I can see that it was because I wouldn't quit using drugs and alcohol in her house, that I didn't treat her very well. Was I dishonest? Was I selfish in my actions? Did I feel fear that she would find out or that she wouldn't love me if she did? Did it cause resentment?

I can go on in my character defect list with this one resentment if I want to be fearless and searching as it suggests. Was I deceitful, bossy, arrogant, angry, gluttonous, depressed, egocentric, compulsive, jealous, lazy, negative, self-centered, liar, insecure? I can go on *ad infinitum*. We all have a lot more than this if we are honest about it.

Ask yourself: *What is a character defect? Who was affected by it?*

Continue to do this with everything except for resentment and fear. When you get to fear, make a new list of everything you fear.

Ask yourself: *What do I fear?*

When you get to resentment, you'll need to ask the following questions:

Ask yourself: *What is the resentment? What is the reason I have it? What is my part in the resentment?*

Then look back at your underlying fear.

Ask yourself: *What is it I expect from this person I resent?*

IDENTIFYING DEEPER ISSUES

Here's another example from my own inventory to help it make sense.

When I started working through the 12 Steps, I realized I had a deep resentment toward my ex-wife. She had left me, and we divorced a few years earlier. I resented that she'd left me when I was so sick. Turned her back on me when I needed her the most. Left me for dead when I was dying, so I thought? Took away our daughter from me. I obtained a court order so I couldn't see or be with her unless it was under supervised visitation. I hated her for this.

My resentment meant I turned to alcohol further. I drank more than ever. Had multiple arrests, DUIs and ended up in jail. I blamed her for all of it. She was the cause of all of my misery. So I thought?

When I had the opportunity to get through this part of my inventory, I was asked hard questions by my sponsor. He said, "What's your part in this?"

I said, "What? You expect me to take the blame for this? She left me; I didn't leave her. She took our daughter from me and wouldn't let me see her!"

He said, "I want to know what your part is?"

He asked. "What is your resentment, Cord?"

I said, "It's my ex-wife. She left me, divorced me, and kept my daughter from me."

"How did you treat her?"

"Not very well, I suppose."

"Was your drinking out of control?"

"Yes, it was."

"Did you love her and treat her well?"

"I did love her, but no, I did not treat her well at all."

"Was she concerned about her safety and the safety of your daughter?"

"Yes, she was terrified of me. She was at her wit's end. She begged me to get help, and I refused."

At the point, I cried, "What have I done?"

I had to be honest with myself about this. Just then, for the first time, I realized that alcohol had turned me into someone my wife didn't know and someone that she feared. Someone that she feared enough that she needed to protect our daughter from me with a court order. For the first time, I faced this heartbreaking reality.

Then he went on to ask more hard questions. "Cord, what was it that you feared the most as a result of her leaving you? What was it that you feared most about her taking your daughter and keeping you away from her?"

I replied, "That my daughter wouldn't love me anymore, I said. That my daughter would fear me like her mother did and wouldn't want anything to do with me. That losing my wife meant that no one would ever love me again. That I would be alone for the rest of my life."

He went on to say, "If you look at the underlying fear in this one resentment, it's your fear of being unloved by your daughter and that you had caused a tremendous amount of pain to your ex-wife that you will never be forgiven for. Am I correct?"

I said, "Yes."

Then I wept. Cried like a little boy. I grieved for days over the pain I had caused them. Facing the pain of this, I had to recognize that instead of owning my part in all of this, I had resented my ex-wife instead. I had already inventoried this issue numerous times in my mind over a couple of years leading up to this before

I finally was able to uncover the truth behind it and deal with it because I had a sponsor who helped me through it in this manner.

This is the way all character defects should be done. It's a searching, fearless, moral inventory of our character defects. The word searching and fearless implies to be willing to explore every nook and cranny of our past, leaving no stone unturned to uncover the issues that are blocking us from direct communication with God and keeping us from a spiritual awakening.

THE EXACT NATURE OF YOUR WRONGDOINGS

Now, you are probably feeling a little squeamish about the idea of having to do this about right now. Let me give you some hope. Going through this little exercise with my sponsor and working together toward the day that I could make direct amends with my daughter and ex-wife for my wrongdoings is, without a doubt, the most liberating thing I have ever experienced.

The people in your life that you fear most have been harmed by you will forgive. They still love you and want the best for you. You see, they know more than anyone, the damage that alcohol and drugs have done to you as a person. And they want you in their lives. My daughter adores her dad, and my ex-wife has, on numerous occasions, made it very clear that she is aware of what I went through. Aware of the difficulties I had and my victory over them. That she wishes me only happiness. Knowing this has given me a lot of freedom and happiness.

The reason it is so important for us to uncover the exact nature of our wrongs is this. Look at the difference between Steps 4 and 5. In Step 4, we are writing down our inventory. Taking stock in our wrongdoings and shortcomings. Finding the truth about ourselves, resentments, and who it has affected. Taking ownership of our part in all of them. In Step 5, we are admitting to God, to ourselves, and to another human being the exact "nature" of these wrongs. The cause and origin of these wrongs.

In Step 5, we find specifics. Specifically, how was I deceitful, resentful, manipulating, dishonest, selfish, and self-centered. Specifically, what was my underlying fear in this? You see, once I got down to the truth about the how and why of it with my ex-wife and daughter. Why I had feared to be unloved because of my wrongdoing, the resentment toward her went away. At that point, I only felt remorse and sorrow for what I had done to them and my other children. The good news, as I said before, is that I was able to deal with this Step 9 and put these issues behind me for good. Step 9 truly set me free! —we will get to this later in the book.

When I was able to clearly see my part. Where had I been self-ish, dishonest, self-seeking, and frightening, then I could look at it from an entirely different angle. I had to look at my part in all of this.

During those years that I harbored this resentment, I hadn't uncovered my part in the exact nature of my wrongdoing. The only way for me to uncover the exact nature of my wrongdoing was to go through a series of questions with someone who had experience in doing an inventory and specifically what questions to ask me. Someone such as a Sponsor who has been through this before.

When we go on to Steps 6 and 7, we need to know these things. Because if we don't discover specifically what we want God to remove when we get to Steps 6 and 7, then how can we expect him to remove them. The reason for this is because there is one spiritual law that God will not violate with us. The law of our freewill.

I needed to know specifically what I wanted God to remove from me. If I didn't bring that fear of not being loved by my daughter to

God in Steps and 6 and 7, and ask him to remove it, then he wasn't going to remove it. That is why you must know specifically what you want him to remove.

So as you go through the inventory. Keep it simple. You can't do this wrong, and if you ask for guidance from your higher power or a God of your understanding, you will find this to be a very straightforward process. If you have questions, review the instructions again. What is most important is that you are willing to face the things within you that are keeping you further away from direct communication with God or a higher power.

This is the end of Step 4. I want to congratulate you for having the courage to complete your inventory. It takes great courage to do this step, so take the opportunity to reflect on it and how your character defects will no longer be a part of who you are and who you will be once you finish the 12 Steps.

IF YOU CAN'T
SEE GOD,
THEN YOU
CAN'T HEAR
HIM EITHER.
IF YOU CAN'T
COMMUNICATE
WITH GOD,
OR A HIGHER POWER,
THEN YOU CAN'T
MOVE FORWARD.

CHAPTER 5

PROMISES, PROMISES

Whoever conceals his transgressions will not prosper,
but he who confesses and forsakes them will obtain mercy.

— PROVERBS 28:13 (ESV)

Step 5 is a very simple and only requires that you have done your earnest to complete the 4th Step and discussed it with a sponsor, counselor, or someone you trust, and God. Step 5 says: "We admitted to God, to ourselves, and to another human being the exact nature of our wrongs."

If you have completed the 4th Step, then move on through Step 5. If you haven't, it would be a good idea to get together with your sponsor and continue working on Step 4 to completion so that you can move on to experience the promises that come from working through the rest of the steps.

The process of this is simple. After talking about your inventory with another human being—such as a sponsor or spiritual leader—then take the same list to God and discuss the exact nature of our wrongs. Talk about your resentments, shortcomings, character defects, and how they have affected others and especially discuss how they have affected you as a person and how it has affected your drinking or using. Then take the inventory list to prayer and discuss it with God or your higher power just as you did with another human being.

Okay, when you have completed Steps 4 and 5, you will be ready to launch right into the next steps. Notice again, just like the authors, I used the word "launch." I didn't say mosey, saunter, waltz, or skip. We need to LAUNCH! We need to move now into our step work with speed, determination, and excitement, or we will lose the momentum. We are going to have some real fun from here on out.

DELVING INTO THE DARKNESS

In Chapter 6 of *Alcoholics Anonymous*, the authors suggest swallowing our pride and going to the task of highlighting every character defect and darkest issues of our past. Once you've finished this 5th Step, you will have withheld nothing from yourself, another human being, and God. You will be able to hold up your head and look the world in the eyes again. You will find peace. Your fears will leave you as you will feel nearer to God. Whatever your spiritual beliefs up to now, you will begin to feel a spiritual experience like you've never had before. Your cravings for alcohol and your problems will begin to fade. You will begin to feel as if you are walking hand in hand in hand with God or the spirit of the universe.

Once we have let go of all of our resentments, our imperfections, shortcomings, and uncovered everything from the darkest part of our past, we will be free. If you get to this point and you aren't feeling satisfied and happy about what you have just completed, then you need to stop here. This is what my sponsor did for me at this point.

He asked me a few questions. After I finished my inventory, he asked if I was happy about what we had done so far, and I said, "Not really."

He asked, "Are you at peace now?"

I said, "Kind of . . ."

He said, "Can you look the world in the eye and hold your head up now?"

I said, "No."

He asked, "Do you feel closer to God?"

I said, "Not as much as I thought I would." And he shut the book!

He shut the book and said, "You have left something out!" He told me to go find it from the darkest nook and cranny of my past, as the book says. I was sure I had covered everything. But I knew better. Honesty was my biggest character defect. So I began again.

A few days went by while as I reworked my inventory. I called up my sponsor and told him I was done. He said, "Did you find it?"

I said, "Yes." It was actually the biggest thing on my list that I was missing. The number-one thing on my inventory list that I had left out because of the fear of facing it was myself.

My fear of failure. The fear of my ability to be honest with me, others, and God. I doubted myself and my ability to stay sober and rebuild my own life. I feared that this worked for everyone else, but wouldn't work for me. I feared that no one would ever love me again because I was an alcoholic. I had not dealt with or talked to God about my fears and my dishonesty.

My sponsor told me to look at what the authors say—"withholding nothing." They don't say, "Hey, Cord, it's okay for you to withhold that one that that you are afraid to face. That one thing that oh, by the way, is your biggest character defect. They don't say, hey, Cord, feel free to leave that out when you talk to God if you want. Don't worry about it, he'll understand." They say, "withholding nothing." Meaning rigorous honesty!

He helped me through this by telling me that because of the promises found in Step 3, I was going to be okay if I had faith and followed this simple proven plan. He said, "Cord, you turned your life and will over to God. He is now your employer. You are his employee. All you need to do is stay sober is ask him every morning, what he needs you to do today? He will give you a set of instructions and everything you need!"

And this is exactly what happened to me. The blessings that have poured down on my head because of these promises are too many for me to count. Not just financially but spiritually and physically, which is much more important to me than money. Every day holds an unfolding miracle in my life. I walk this Earth a happy, free, and joyous man because of these promises and because I was willing to do the work.

Without exception, every person I take through the Steps has had the same experience as I did if they were willing to do the work. They get to this point, and I ask them the same questions my sponsor asked me, and they have the same result. It is not easy facing the darkest parts of our past. Not easy writing it down and certainly more difficult talking to someone else about it.

CLOSER TO GOD

It also says that we feel closer to our Creator having done the 4th Step. This has been my experience too. For the first time in my sobriety, I began to feel closer to God. Closer than I had ever been. I knew this process had given me that direct line to God. Finally, he was picking up every time I called. It has continued to be this way for me ever since.

My new found connection with God changed me. It will change you too. You will find that the questionable things about you will fade and disappear. Look at it this way. You might be a dishonest, no good horse thief, but the closer to you get to God, the more damned uncomfortable it will be to keep stealing horses.

It was the first time that I had ever been able to talk to another human being about all of the things that were troubling me and free myself from every one of them. All the pain I had caused others—the lies, deceit, and trouble. These are the things that had been keeping me from being closer to God.

What the authors said were true for me. When I was able to share these things with another person, I began to feel delighted and free. I started to feel perfect peace and ease with myself and my surroundings. My sponsor was correct. If you aren't delighted and at perfect peace, once you have gone through this process, you are probably leaving something out. Probably one of the most important things about your past that need to be talked about.

In the last part, the authors say that we are walking hand in hand with the spirit of the universe. If you do experience this, as I did after completing my 5th Step, I would suggest that you share this experience with someone. Take your experience to meetings and share them with others. It will give you more freedom and security in your sobriety. This is difficult for some. It was difficult for me as well at first. Sharing my feelings at a meeting just didn't feel natural to me. But the more I did it, the better I felt.

I can tell you that going through the 12 Steps like they were done in the 1940s is going to be different for you than for most people. This is what happened to me. My sponsor took me through the steps very quickly and without hesitation. We worked daily for about four days until I was done.

As I described in the Introduction, you can't take anyone through these steps too quickly. Especially if you are like me. You see, I am the real alcoholic that we talk about. I was sicker than most. That means that I needed to get through the 12 Steps as quickly as possible. I needed to get to the promises they held. I needed to get to power as fast as possible. I needed real POWER!

Once I was shown the 12 Steps in this way, my sobriety started to look very different for me. I had people all around me with a lot more sobriety than I had that were struggling to stay sober. In and out of the program, just like I was for so long. They were still working on their 4th Step at six months, a year, or even two years into sobriety. I believe this to be because they had sponsors that had their own interpretation of the way the 12 Steps were to be done. Somewhere along the way, we lost sight of how simple and successful it was for the pioneers of the program in the 1940s. We decided to fix something that wasn't broken.

Sponsors started telling newcomers things like, "You can't work on your 4th Step until you've been six months sober." "It's going to take you a year of hard work to get all the way through the 12 Steps, and your chances of making it are slim to none!" Or: "You shouldn't sponsor anyone until you have been sober for at least a year."

Where is any of this written in Alcoholics Anonymous? Where does it outline such demands? I have never found it. Remember what I said at the beginning: Are you willing to consider that if it isn't written in the Big Book, it isn't in the 12 Steps? If these kinds of outlandish statements had been included, the program would have failed from the very beginning.

Just to be clear. My understanding of this doesn't make me better or smarter than any of these people in any way. I'm not here to debate or tell you that I know these steps more than the next person. It just gives sobriety a whole new look for me. I feel different than I did before. Because once I had gone all the way through the 12 Steps as they did in the 1940s, the compulsion to drink was removed from me. I was free from my addiction. Remember what the authors wrote about what you should do after completing the 5th Step?

Carefully review your work and what you have done so far. Go home, find a quiet place, and thank God from the bottom of your heart after we finish the 5th Step for knowing Him better.

They suggest a careful review of the first five steps and to ask the following question.

Ask yourself: *Have I left anything out? Is my work solid so far? Have I missed something important?*

GOING HOME TO PRAY

Notice they wrote that we went home to pray. It says we went to find a quiet place to thank God from the bottom of our hearts that we know him better at this point. It doesn't say we forgot about our work for a while and went fishing. It doesn't say we took off for Disneyland and forgot about the work we have done so far. No, it says we immediately go to a quiet place to tell God how much we love and appreciate him and to thank him for doing this for us.

I realized at this point in my work that if I truly wanted to be free from alcohol, then I needed to follow these instructions and complete this step just as it is outlined.

To do this the right way, you need to follow what is written in *Alcoholics Anonymous*, so let's take the first five steps and turn them into YES or NO questions:

Thinking about the first five steps, answer the following questions YES or NO:

Step 1: *Have I admitted that I have no power? Have I admitted that my life is unmanageable?*
YES/NO

Step 2: *Have I come to believe there is a power greater than I can restore me to sanity?*
YES/NO

Step 3: *Have I made a decision to turn my will and my life over to the care of God as I understand him/her/it?*
YES/NO

Step 4: *Have I made a fearless and moral inventory omitting nothing?*
YES/NO

Step 5: *Have I admitted to myself, God, and another person the exact nature of my wrongs?*
YES/NO

Congratulations on completing Step 5.

YOU MIGHT BE
A DISHONEST,
NO GOOD
HORSE THIEF,
BUT THE CLOSER
YOU GET TO GOD,
THE MORE DAMNED
UNCOMFORTABLE
IT WILL BE TO KEEP
STEALING HORSES.

CHAPTER 6

READY OR NOT HERE I COME

God doesn't fix my problems; he fixes my thinking.
Then my problems fix themselves.

—R. CORD BEATTY

Step 6 is a quick and easy experience and is about preparing for Step 7. The authors wrote that if I am satisfied with my work, I should be ready to ask God to remove all the objectionable things in my life—anything that is blocking us from God, including character defects

Ask yourself: *Am I willing to let God take these things from me? Am I ready to let God remove all of them?*

Step 6 is not actually doing it. Just preparing ourselves.

Some more questions to ask: *Does God really have the power to take them all? Does God have all the power? Is God everything, or is He is nothing at all? Can He take them all from me if I ask?*

Getting ready is the essence of Step 6. The 7th Step prayer was written only as a suggestion. If you feel you are ready, then look at Step 7 and make your request:

Humbly ask God to remove your shortcomings.

STEP 7 PRAYER

This prayer can be done in any way that feels comfortable to you. Here is a suggestion that I've used for myself:

> *God, I am now willing to give myself to you, all of me good and bad. I ask that you remove all of my character defects, which stand in the way of my usefulness to you, and that is blocking me from direct communication with you. Please give me the knowledge to know your will for me, and the power to carry it out. Please give me strength as I move forward to do the work you ask of me.*
> *Amen*

Note that the authors wrote "all of me" in the prayer. Not just some or a piece of me. They say, "all of me." This is why you need to be very specific about what you're asking God to remove.

When I went through this, there was one thing I kept glossing over—my compulsiveness. As with most alcoholics and addicts, the compulsion to use is always the biggest issue. My compulsiveness was probably one of my biggest character defects. Watching my car drive itself into the liquor store parking lot over and over again. Finding myself standing in line with a bottle of alcohol without thinking it through. Going home and, without hesitation, drinking until I passed out. Swearing to myself the next day that I wouldn't do that again and then doing the same thing that night. Repeating the madness of this over and over again with no end.

I know now that one of the reasons I spent years suffering, in and out of AA, drinking, having relapse after relapse is because I never asked God to remove the compulsion to drink alcohol from me for good. I had asked him to remove my selfishness, dishonesty, self-seeking, fears, and resentments. But I never took the time to ask him to remove my compulsion to drink for good. Maybe it's because I was praying with some reservations?

Have you experienced rambling prayers when you pray? I know sometimes I've prayed because I know I need to talk or feel somewhat lost—but don't know quite what to say. I know I need to ask for something, but I just don't really make a specific point. If you don't know specifically what it is that you want God to remove from you, then how can he? And it doesn't mean asking when he is going to remove it. Our job is not to ask him *when* but *what*. Our job is to specifically ask what we want him to remove. We need to let him decide when is the best time to take that from us.

Have you ever heard someone say, "If you've completed the 4th Step, you should burn it or throw it away"?

Why would you do this? You may need to reference it again as you work through the steps.

Have you ever told yourself that you are working on your defects? Or heard someone else say the same. I've heard that many times. "I've been working on my 4th Step for three years." If you are like me, the more I work on my defects, the worse they become. I need them dealt with and put behind me now!

Your job isn't to work on your defects. It is to identify them and ask God to remove all of them. Keep it simple. If you're working on them, you are playing God. If you find yourself doing this, you're still trying to manage your defects and your disease. Still trying to manage your unmanageable life. Doing this only embellishes your defects and makes them worse. It is impossible to continue to work on your defects if you're applying these simple spiritual principles, identifying what you need removed and asking. Does this make sense?

WORKING THROUGH STEPS 6 AND 7

Okay. Now we should be ready to move through Steps 6 and 7 together. So I ask you to come up with your own prayer or use my example. If you are willing to so. If you are willing to let God remove these things that have been keeping you from being close to him, then let's do this step now.

God, I am now willing to give myself to you, all of me good and bad. I ask that you remove all of my character defects, which stand in the way of my usefulness to you, and that is blocking me from direct communication with you. Please give me the knowledge to know your will for me, and the power to carry it out. Please give me strength as I move forward to do the work you ask of me.
Amen

Congratulations, you have now completed Steps 6 and 7.

YOUR JOB ISN'T
TO WORK ON
YOUR DEFECTS.
IT IS TO
IDENTIFY THEM
AND ASK GOD
TO REMOVE
ALL OF THEM.
KEEP IT SIMPLE.

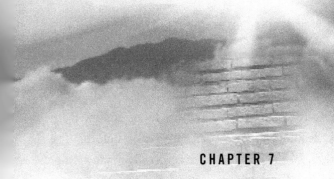

CHAPTER 7

MAKING A LIST AND CHECKING IT TWICE

Humility leads to strength and not to weakness. It is the highest form of self-respect to admit mistakes and to make amends for them.

—JOHN J. MCCLOY

S tep 8 asks you to do the following:

> *Make a list of all persons you have harmed and be willing to make amends to them all.*

And then Step 9 asks you to:

Make direct amends to such people wherever possible,
except when to do so would injure them or others.

You've probably read about the need for more action. Faith without work is dead. Have you ever heard this before? The authors suggest that, for the most part, we've already made a list of people we had harmed due to our character defects when we completed the inventory in the 4th Step. So if you haven't thrown away it, you already have your amends list. You know who you need to make your amends to. It goes without saying that you've exposed yourself to a drastic self-appraisal in the 4th Step, so now you can clean up the wreckage of your past.

The authors suggest that you start by sweeping and cleaning your side of the street. If you aren't ready to make certain amends, then you ask God until you are ready. Some amends take longer and require more effort than others, but you must do them all. Remember that you've agreed to do anything to conquer your addictions. This is important because saying, "I will repair the damage I've done in the past" means that "I am now going to go forth and attempt to correct the wrongs that I have caused others in my past."

The authors describe the real purpose of cleaning up the past is to get to a place in your life to be of maximum service to God and others. In other words, to be "spiritually fit." This is also the real purpose of the 12 Steps. Becoming sober is just part of it.

FINDING PURPOSE
AND MAKING A PLAN

When I started the 12 Steps, I didn't have a purpose. I had no plan. I didn't know what I was going to do. It wasn't until I worked through the steps with my sponsor that I learned my real purpose on Earth.

The authors wrote that you need to have a sincere desire to right our wrongs. You need to be willing and committed toward this process and not just keep talking about it. It means being eager to right the wrongs. To make amends, you have to think, "How can I approach someone I hated?" The authors wrote that the person may have done more wrong to us than we did to them. You may have a desire to right the wrong but may have difficulty admitting your faults or your part.

Even if this is the case, you must take the bull by the horns and get to it. You may not like it, but you must do it if you want to be free from addiction. To do this, I recommend you approach this person with humility, love, and forgiveness in your heart. Take responsibility for your part and express your regrets. Then ask if there is anything you can do to make things right?

It was my experience that the words that kept coming up for me at this point were dishonesty, selfishness, and my ego. It meant that I needed to go back through my inventory list of every person that I had affected with these character defects and make direct amends to them if I was going to find freedom from my addiction. This was something that I didn't want to do. Making amends is never fun. Especially to some of the folks in my life. Nevertheless, I went about this in the same manner as the book described: I made my list. I carefully decided how and where I was going to make my amends and then I went to it.

There was one man that I struggled with making amends to. Years ago, I had borrowed money from him when I was about to lose my house to foreclosure. At that time, he was a great friend and loaned me the money, and when I couldn't pay it back, he made my life a living hell. He harassed my family and me. Showed up at our house unannounced, uninvited, and openly professed his entitlement to intrude in our family affairs. I became very resentful toward him as time went on.

On one occasion, he came to my house on July 4th when my family was out in the front yard celebrating with fireworks. He came down our long driveway in his four-wheel-drive pickup truck with its huge lights lit up—blinding us and ruining our fireworks fun. Having drunk a lot of alcohol that night, I erupted in anger and made a huge scene. I told him I never wanted to see him or hear from him again.

Rather than face him, I would tell people about how he was selfish and arrogant behind his back. How he had all the money in the world but wouldn't help others who really needed it. I had completely forgotten that he had really helped me when I needed it. I was so embarrassed and ashamed that I quit talking to him and ruined our friendship. I was sure he had long written off the debt and probably me too in the process. I was so selfish and arrogant that I stayed away from him and his family for years. This was one of the hardest amends for me to make.

I finally humbled myself and got up the courage to see him. I drove to his house and sat in the car for the longest time. I prayed for the right outcome, walked up to the door, and knocked. He opened the door and snapped, "What do you want?" With hat in hand, I admitted that I was wrong in treating him badly and talking about him the way that I had done all those years.

When I got to the part about asking him for his forgiveness and asked him if there was anything that I could offer to make it right with him, he stared into my eyes for what seemed like an uncomfortable eternity and then said, "Oh, what the hell Cord? Don't worry about it, you know the money doesn't mean anything to me," then he laughed out loud. He continued, "Watching you crawl up to my doorstep on your hands and knees like this is enough for me. That was priceless!" and he laughed out loud some more. I laughed right along with him. It was hilarious! He asked me inside, and we hugged. Since then, we have become closer friends than we ever were.

What I didn't know was that during those years, he had stopped drinking, became active in his church, and had gone through the same experiences I was having with the 12 Steps. It had worked for him as well.

THE VALUE OF AMENDS

It is so important not to take this part of the process too seriously. We have to maintain that there are levity and relief in doing these steps and making our amends. Remember this: we are there for one reason only. We aren't there to debate or talk about our past mistakes. We are there to make a statement of our intent and purpose, take full responsibility, and ask for permission to make things right, if possible. That's it!

You see, you can't have this kind of experience if you don't do the steps. The relief of making amends with those we've wronged will bring freedom and peace to your heart. And those that you thought would never forgive you, will.

Under no condition do we argue or criticize. We don't debate the other person's part in the amends. That's not why we are there. We are there to take responsibility for our part only. We tell the other person that we may not be able to stop drinking unless we clean up our past. We are there to sweep our side of the street only! We don't tell the other person what they should do in this situation. We just make our amends in a calm, humble, and open manner, and when done, we will be satisfied with our results.

And we aren't out there to talk about the person who we owe the amends to. We aren't there to talk about their faults. When we make and amend, we are there for one purpose only: to make a direct amend to the individual we have harmed. That's it!

If you're making an amend with someone and then follow up with, "Oh, by the way, there are some things about you that I need to discuss with you." This doesn't work. You will undo all of the goodwill of making the amend in the first place.

SWEEPING YOUR SIDE OF THE STREET

This isn't how the authors describe it, they say, "We are there to sweep off our side of the street." This means you are there for one reason and one reason only. Regardless of the outcome. It doesn't matter if the other person rejects the amend. You have swept your side of the street clean. You aren't there to talk about the other person's faults.

The person you're making amends with needs to know you're doing this for a specific reason. Because you need to clear your conscience so things can be right him or her and with God to be free. It doesn't matter if they don't accept your amends. You're not there to make them happy. To get an atta-boy! To get them to praise you for making amends. You are there for only that one reason: you'll be clear after you make it. If you don't do this with the right motive, things will backfire.

There is a right way and a wrong way to make an amends. The authors tell us that there is specific things that should be included in a properly written amends.

- I make a statement as to why I am here; *"I am here to make a direct amends to you for the wrongs I have committed."*
- I ask for their permission to make the amends; *"Are you open to hearing this amends from me?"*
- I take full responsibility for my actions or my part; *"I deeply regret the things that I have done that have hurt you in the past."*
- I ask for permission to make things right; *"If there is anything that I can do to right the wrongs I have committed against you, I would very much like the opportunity to do so."*

One of the biggest amends on my list was to my ex-wife. I didn't know exactly how I was going to accomplish making an amend for all of the wrongs I'd committed and hurt I'd caused over the years. I decided to write her a letter instead of doing it in person. I wrote out this long graceful, poetic, and, in my own mind, "epic" amends letter. One that would free me and forever burn into her memory that I am actually a good guy. So I thought?

This was for me the one big amend that needed to be done. So I sent an email. I started out with such grace and said: "I have turned my life and will over to my Creator, and I am now a grateful and sober man. I am working very hard every day to make my amends and work through my steps so that I can remain free from alcohol."

I went on to outline the amends and then humbly asked her for forgiveness and if there was any way for me to the right the wrongs. However, at the beginning of the amends after my statement on remaining free from alcohol, I added the following before moving on: "I hope you understand where I am coming from. There are always two sides to every story, and we both have faults, right? I just wanted to let you know that I am sorry for the things I have done that have hurt you." At the end of my email, I said: "Call me some time, we should probably talk this over."

I received back only one word from the email. It said, "Okay???"

My reaction was, "Oh, you bitch!" That's it? After all that? Five pages of pouring my heart out. How could you not acknowledge how hard this was for me? How could you be so incredibly selfish?"

What did I do? Fingers blazing, I wrote an even bigger disaster than the first one, and then without thinking it through, I hit send!

Then I said to myself, "Shit! What have I done?" I just sat there starring at the computer screen: "Oh, oh, oh, no, no, no! What have I done?"

I whined and complained to my sponsor, who quickly pointed out a few things I missed. He asked me to read the amends to him. I read the first few paragraphs until I got the part where I said, "There are always two sides to every story, and we both have faults."

He said, "Stop! Don't read anymore to me, she didn't."

The light bulbs went on. I was the selfish one. This was all my own doing. Wow, did I screw this one up! Now I have to go back and make an amend for the amends. Just perfect.

This time I made making my amends very short. Very straightforward. After humbly asking her to please disregard the first and second emails, I wrote: "I am aware of every single thing that that I have done that has hurt you during our 17-year marriage. I know that I have hurt you deeply on many occasions. I take full responsibility for all of it, and I regret everything I have done. I need to do this if I am going to stop drinking for good. If there is any way I can ever do anything that would right the wrongs I have done to you, I will welcome the opportunity to do so." I left it at that.

A few weeks later, I received back a well-written email. It didn't criticize me or put me down. Instead, it read: "Thank you. I hope you find your happiness. It's all I ever wanted for you."

Her email went on to talk about all of the good things she saw in me over all those years. The memories of our family, raising our children together, the laughter, and just how close our family was for years. It didn't talk about any of the bad times or my alcoholism. I wept quietly as I read the words, understanding for the first time what it meant by sweeping my side of the street. The freedom that comes from doing this work. What true forgiveness felt like and what it meant to be free at last! For the first time in my life, I was truly experiencing the power of God.

MAKING AMENDS TO CREDITORS AND DEBTORS

You're likely to have money and creditor problems—as is usual for most recovering alcoholics and addicts. If you do, don't make any excuses for your difficulties and take full responsibility for your actions. You must place great importance on facing your creditors to the right our wrongs. No matter how much fear you might have about facing creditors and righting these wrongs, you must make an effort. If you don't, you'll most likely unwind all of the progress you have made.

A business partner and I owed money to a man in California from whom we had borrowed a large sum of money and never paid back. This man had pursued me over a long period. He harassed me by text, email, and phone. Letters came from him and his wife over the years, threatening legal actions against me. The collection efforts were focused on me and not on my business partner. He even went as far as to post messages on social media sites that I owed him money and to never lend me money. He was relentless in his pursuit. Usually showing up every few months to make some form of demand. I had grown to resent this man. I resented him to the point that I often thought that even if I could repay the debt, I wouldn't out of spite and resentment toward him.

I went to my sponsor about this issue on my amends list. I

told him of my resentment toward this man and his wife for all of the things they had said about me and that I didn't want to make amends to either one of them. He said this to me, "How free do you want to be? Are you willing to do anything to be free from alcohol and addiction?" I said yes and knew what had to be done from there.

I attempted calling this man and his wife, but they wouldn't take the call or just didn't answer. I took this issue to God in prayer, asking for the best outcome and to guide my thoughts and words in this matter. Then I wrote a letter to them concerning my eight-year-old debt. This is what it said:

Dear Bob,

I hope that life finds you well and happy these days. I have had you on my mind now for some time. I have been sober now for several years and have opened an inpatient treatment center for alcohol and drug addiction. Our business helps those who need my help finding sobriety and connection with God.

The reason I am writing to you is that it has come to my attention that I owe you heartfelt amends. When I needed you and your help, you were always there for me. You and your wife helped me financially and emotionally when I needed you the most. I have let this issue fall by the wayside for a long period, without facing the issue that my actions damaged our friendship. For this, I am deeply regretful. I love you and will always be forever grateful for the help and support you gave me when I needed you.

If there is any way that I can make right the things that I have done that have hurt you, I will welcome the opportunity to do so. I don't make very much money doing what I do, as you can imagine. Most of the time, I find myself giving away more than I take in. But I can offer to repay you a little each month if you would accept it from me.

Cord

It is important to point out that I referred only to myself and didn't include my business partner. We had both borrowed the money, but this part of my journey wasn't about my business partner. It was about me. This was my amends, not his. There was no reason to bring him into this. I was sweeping my side of the street, not his. I needed to do this for my sobriety. The answer I received from this amends was astonishing and not what I expected. It read:

Dear Cord,

I am thrilled that you have found peace and purpose in your life. There is nothing better than to look in the mirror each morning, knowing that you are helping your fellow man. There is no higher calling than to give of yourself, your love, and your gentle spirit in helping others find their way. I deeply admire what you are doing, and my prayer would be that you find the courage and the resources to continue.

I forgive you completely! I also believe that there should be some repayment in these matters, so I offer this suggestion. As to the amount, it is not important as the work you do. So just apply any amount you were thinking of sending me each month for this debt to those you serve in hopes that it helps them through their difficulties. The amount may be something that you might not have been able to afford at the time you give it, but you do it anyway. I am so proud and happy for you in all that you are doing, God bless you, my friend,

Bob

Again, I wept as I read the return letter. I believe that the forgiveness I received from making amends is one of the greatest gifts God has ever given me. I am a free man because of this and so many other amends and responses like this that I've received. I don't have to live my life looking over my shoulder. You will find that you will have this experience as well.

Almost every amends that you make will be met with the same

type of result if you ask God to guide and direct you in the process. You see, most people are genuinely good. It was us that had the defects of character, not them. By doing your amends in earnest and sincerity, you will find that you will be free from the crosses you carry through life as you clean up your side of the street.

GETTING CREATIVE WITH MAKING AMENDS

The authors wrote about innumerable forms of reparations. They wrote that you must make a decision to go to any lengths to find your spiritual experience. They suggest you pray and ask for strength and direction when offering amends, even if it causes you a great deal of discomfort. It must be done no matter what.

Notice they say, "innumerable forms." This means that there are multiple ways of making amends. Working with your sponsor can assist you in making your amends—even if you need to get quite creative to do so.

For example, I found myself in a very precarious situation with an early sponsor. I admired him very much, and he helped me tremendously. While he was sponsoring me, and working with me, I had a relapse and drank again after four years of consistent sobriety.

I remember some of the conversations I had with him about this. I was drinking, and he said, "You aren't ready to be sober, Cord." I erupted in anger and lashed out at him, calling him a fraud and a phony and to never call me again.

My relapse lasted but a day or so, and then I picked myself up, took the bit in my mouth, and moved on. However, now I had a bigger problem than just relapse. I had lost one of the best sponsors I'd ever had due to my selfish, dishonest, decision to drink again. Over the next few years, this was an issue that really bothered me.

I was sober, working the steps, making my amends, and needed to make amends to him.

I attempted to call him, but by then, his number had changed. I had his email, but I really wanted to speak with him directly. I had been told that he had moved to another state. A sponsor I was working with at the time suggested that I write a letter to him addressing it to general delivery to the town I believed he was living in. I listened to this suggestion and thought this was a great idea. The letter went unanswered.

I thought at the time that I had done my part. Swept my side of the street. I went to my sponsor and told him what I had done and that I felt good about it. He said, "Hold on just a minute, Cord. If you really wanted to get in touch with this man, you would do it."

He said, "You know what town he lives in. I would bet you that a dozen or more meetings are going on in that town, and he attends every one of them. If you really want to find him, you will."

"Are you serious?" I asked? "I'm expected to drive, fly, go, and search out every meeting hall until I find him?"

He was very serious and said, "How free to you want to be?" I knew right then and there what I had to do.

Needless to say, I did put a lot of work into this. It took me weeks to find him and make my amends. The response was one of understanding. He understood the importance of what I had just done. He thanked me, and I left with a clear conscience and a sense of freedom.

Here is another example of being creative with amends. I never had the opportunity to make an amends to my mother before she died. I know my behavior and actions hurt her in the past. I never had the opportunity to right the wrongs I had done.

As time went on, this issue began to kick me in the ass! There were nights I couldn't sleep over this. This amends was one would not leave me alone. I knew that unless I could find a solution, I might drink again.

I took the issue to a mentor and spiritual advisor. I confided in him that I could not find a solution. I told him in detail of the wrongs I had committed and the way I had hurt my mother in the past. He suggested a solution I couldn't see.

He asked me to write the amends to my mother and discuss it with him before I did anything. He then asked me if I trusted God. I told him with all my heart. He said; "God has mail service Cord." This made perfect sense!

I took some time, meditated on what I was asking for, knelt down and read the amends to God. Then I humbly asked if he would deliver it to my mother. I have no doubt in my mind that my amends was hand delivered and well received. I was free once again!

The point is this:

There are many ways to make amends. You have to be willing to go to any length for your freedom from addiction. The importance of taking full responsibility for yourself and your actions and not the actions of anyone else is what sets you free.

TAKING FULLY RESPONSIBILITY

The authors talk about never bringing someone else into the amends and placing blame on them in an attempt to make amends. It won't work. What the authors are saying is that you need to be mindful and considerate of others who may be affected by the amends. Step 9 says, "Made direct amends." So think about what you are doing before jumping in with both feet.

Is this amends going to cause more harm, and if so, do I make an amend to that person? In other words, don't make amends just to relieve yourself of a burden, guilt, and shame if it will hurt the person you are making amends to or someone else. The authors suggest that before taking drastic measures involving other people, you need to ask for their consent. If you receive their consent, consult with God and others, then you can make amends.

In the case of our man who had abused his wife, and went to jail. He needed to make amends in some fashion or form to his ex-wife to be free. For him to make amends directly without harming her husband and children, he would first need to approach the husband and ask for his permission. You see the predicament it would place him in?

So you need to think through each amend before making it.

Ask yourself:

- *Are others going to be hurt when I make these amends?*
- *Have I thought this through?*
- *Have I obtained permission?*
- *Have I prayed about it asking only for the best outcome?*
- *Have I talked to my sponsor about the amends?*
- *Is my amends well planned out?*

If you've followed this process, then you are ready to make the amend and then place the outcome in God's hands. This takes us back to Step 3 when you turned your will over to God and promised to do his will and work. What does that mean? It means cleaning up the wreckage of the past so you can better do God's will and leave the outcome of in his hands so that you can be free.

I didn't know the outcome when I made an amends to my ex-wife. I left that up to God and he took care of it for me. The outcome of that amends was far beyond anything that I had imagined it would be. I didn't know the outcome when I made the amends to Bob and his wife—I left that up to God. I didn't worry about whether or not they would forgive me and leave me alone or continue to pursue me. I didn't know. I left that in God's hands. I didn't know if my past sponsor would understand and forgive me. I knew this had to be done with searching fearless effort on my part and left the rest in God's hands.

It happened each and every time like this for me because I did this in humility, and turned the outcome over to God just as the authors instruct us to do in chapter 6 of the Big Book. In my sobriety, there has never been an unreasonable request from someone I've made amends to, providing that my motives were clear, sincere, and I humbly went to them.

As you are around sober people more and continue to attend meetings, you will hear other alcoholics and addicts say that they only thing they need to do in life is to stay sober one day at a time. Staying sober isn't enough. It is a long way from making right the wrongs you have committed to others. Making right the wrongs you have committed to others will set you free and create long term sobriety. Not just sobriety one day at a time.

Just like me, every person I have ever known who has worked through the 12 Steps and found sobriety, but then drank or used again did so for one reason. It has never been my experience that I drank again because I stopped going to meetings or stopped talking to my sponsor. It was always because I hadn't completed this part of the step work and stopped praying. I stopped communicating with my Creator daily.

I've never met anyone that has relapsed after finishing all 12 Steps, that has not done so for two very good reasons. First, because of something in their past that they haven't faced and made amends for. And second, because they stopped talking to God.

I've developed a conscience from working the steps and making amends. If I am a real alcoholic, which I am. If I am going to drink no matter what because I don't have the power to stop. If I engage in dishonest behavior or stop working on the steps. Stop making my amends. If I stop talking to God, then I am probably going to drink again because I am a real alcoholic, and I can only stand the pain of life for so long before I need to do something about it.

The authors wrote about the long road ahead. They say you must take the lead. Not expecting someone else to do the work. I have used this excuse too many times; "I will just shoot them an text to their phone." We have to think this through and ask: "Did I commit the harm via text?"

In the early parts of Steps 8 and 9, the authors talk about gaining consent before making an amend.

Ask yourself: *When I make an amend, have I asked for permission to make an amend?*

If you see someone on the street that you owe an amend to, are you going to run up and say, "Hey, buddy? Hang on a minute, I owe you an amend?"

No, you're going to approach them calmly and with humility and say, "Hello, John, you've been on my mind for a long time. I would like to make an amend with you if you're open to hearing it from me?"

What if they say, "No, I'm not open to hearing about this?" Does this mean you have to wait for a later date and time to make an amend to him? No, you made an effort to make a direct amend. Your side of the street is clean, and you move on to the next one.

If they say yes, then you're going to ask them a few questions. This is very important when you make amends. To ask the other person how they would like to hear this from you. Now, letter or at a different time when it's convenient for them? Give them this opportunity. It will mean more to them in the long run.

As an example, I sent an email to a woman I had hurt deeply asking for permission to make amends. After gaining permission and willingness to listen, I asked her how she would like to receive it—in person, email, or phone? She emailed me a few days later and thanked me for making this effort and said she would prefer not to talk to me again but would accept it via letter or email. I sent it via email.

Moving on, keep in mind that spiritual life is not just a theory. You have to be living a spiritual life as we read in Chapter 6 of the Big Book. The authors suggest considering "living the steps." Not working on them but living them.

You probably realize that some of your wrongs can't be made right—this is always the case. If this is true, don't worry about them if you can say honestly that you would right the wrong if you could. For some, you might send a letter and leave it at that.

There is also sometimes a very valid reason to postpone the amends. But don't if you can avoid the delay. Approach this step with humility and plan your words carefully. The authors wrote, as God's children we stand on our feet with our head held high. We don't crawl before anyone!

What if you have put much effort into locating someone and you find that can't get in touch with the person you need to make the amend with? Do you just forget about it and write it off?

In this case, make a written and mental note that you can't find or haven't yet found a way to make, the amend directly or indirectly. Then if the person or place presents itself in the future, you can quickly make the amend and move on. This is also an opportunity for you to see just how far and at what length you will go to be free.

BEING AMAZED

I first read about the 9th Step promise years ago. I was amazed at the statement of hope found these words:

"If I am thorough about this stage of my progress halfway through, I will be amazed!"

How cool is this? The authors aren't saying you are going to be amazed before you get halfway through our work. They are clearly stating that you will be amazed when you are halfway through.

The 9th Step promise tells you that you'll find freedom. That you'll find happiness. You won't hold on to regrets or shut the door on your past. You will experience peace and serenity. It won't matter how much suffering you have been through, you will be interested in sharing your experiences with others. Feelings of selfishness and self-pity will disappear, and you will be interested in helping others. Life will change. Fears will leave you. You will instinctively handle circumstances that used to baffle you. You will realize that God is now doing for you what you couldn't do for yourself. These promises will be realized as long as you work for them.

One of the greatest things I've experienced in my sobriety has been watching the guys I sponsor or the people coming through my treatment center. Watching that magical shining light go on and seeing them change. Watching the happiness and joy of God's grace come into their lives. The peace and serenity they gain from it. A big part of this light comes from making amends.

For example, one of the issues I had in my youth was prejudice to homosexuality. I made fun of anyone who was LGBT, criticized them, called them names. I was prejudiced against them. I told my sponsor about this and that I was wrong and that I was sorry but had no way to make amends to this many people. This was an issue that I struggled with, but my sponsor understood just how to handle it when the situation presented itself.

We were sitting in a restaurant one morning where there was also a young man having breakfast with three friends. One of the others was a male, the other two females. I could tell that he and some of his friends were obviously LGBT. They were busy enjoying each other's company and friendship. My sponsor said, "No time like the present Cord. Let's roll!"

I really didn't want to do it, but I did it anyway. I approached these young men and women and made my amends. I introduced myself and stated that I needed to make an amends to them for something I had done in my past. I asked them if they would be open to hearing it from me. One of them said yes. I said that I am a grateful sober man today, and over the years, I had harmed a lot of gay and lesbian people. I told them that I was wrong for doing so. I said I know that every one of us are God's children and that I had no business judging any of them for who they are. I humbly asked them if there was anything I could offer to the right the wrongs that I had done and then offered to pay for their meals.

To my surprise, they all started grinning from ear to ear. Here were four people in front of me, perfect strangers, all having an amazing spiritual experience with me. One of them spoke up and said, "Three of us are recovered addicts and alcoholics as well. We are also grateful members of AA. God has already forgiven you Cord, and we all do too."

I stood there and wept in gratitude. These four individuals, perfect strangers, stood up to gather around me and embrace me with love. I walked away from a free man once again.

This was one of the most amazing experiences in my life. I would doubt that anyone of those people had ever heard anything like this from someone that wasn't LGBT. This was one of the things that truly changed me. Because of this experience, some of the closest friends I have in this life are LGBT, and I am proud to call them my friends, and I love each and every one of them.

Without the 9th Step promise, this truly amazing, healing, spiritual experience would never have happened. It was a miracle for me that I could only experience in the 12 Steps and by making amends.

I promise you this. It has been my experience that if you do the work and are willing to go to any length to be free from your disease, you will have these kinds of experiences.

Ask yourself: *How free do I want to be? What length am I willing to go for freedom?*

THE DOS AND DON'TS OF MAKING AMENDS

I would like to recap how not to make an amend and then go over how to make an amend.

1. The first thing is to gain consent, then depending on the circumstances, ask the person how they would like me to make amends—in person, in writing, or on the phone.

2. If the person is in front of you, ask them if you can make the amend right then.

3. Then take responsibility for your actions. Tell the person that you were wrong. Not just saying that you're sorry because this isn't making an amend. Sorry is an empty word that means nothing. An amend is an attempt at making right the wrongs that you have done directly with the other person.

4. Then ask for their permission to let this issue go. The question is: Is there anything I can do to right this wrong with you?

Now let's explore how not to make an amend. Let's say you owe an amend to one of your friends for being angry and short-tempered with them.

For this purpose, his name is Steve. So you say, "Hey Steve, come over here. I owe you an amend for being rude and yelling at you. I am sorry, but I had a really hard day yesterday, and my boss yelled at me, then the power got turned off at my house, so I had to run home to get it back on. Then the dog ran away, and I had to chase him around the neighborhood for hours. Then my ex-wife called and yelled at me, and it really set me off. Then I ran to the store to get some things I needed, and I ran out of gas and had to hitchhike to get gas. And then my girlfriend said she wants to break up with me. My life is a shit show, Steve. You know what I'm saying? Anyway Steve, I am sorry okay?"

When making an amend, don't offer reasons, excuses, or explanations about your actions. You shouldn't tell the person about your feelings and what is going on in your life. Don't say, "I owe you amends for being such a jackass and then follow with'; "But I need you to understand why I am such a jackass." This isn't the purpose of making amends.

Let me give you an example of how to make proper amends. Let's use Steve again.

"Hello, Steve. I have an amend I would like to make to you. Would you be open to hearing it from me? The other day I spoke harshly to you. I want you to know that I was very wrong for doing that, and I regret it. I would like to know if there is anything I can to do right this wrong with you and if so, I would very much like the opportunity to do so?"

When you make and amend this way, you don't launch into any other conversation with Steve. You don't add to your amends by saying, "By the way, Steve, I have issues with you too that I'd like to talk to about while we are at it." If I do have any other issues with Steve, then I save that for another time. This isn't about Steve's issues, it's about yours.

BECOMING FREE

Step 9 will set you free. It will allow you to walk with your head held high. In my opinion, without Step 9, you will not fully recover. Being sober is not enough. Sober is just the middle ground somewhere between misery and recovery. Amends are difficult to make, and most of the time, you won't like making them. But it will free you. They will become easier to do once you get started.

My sponsor told me to make a list of people I had harmed on a notepad or a 3x5 card and list the individual and the harm I had done. Each page or card gets one harm and one person listed on it. This way, your amends work is no longer guesswork. You don't have to put more time into remembering if you have the amend or not. Once you've done it, you can either tear out the paper or throw away the notecard, and then you are done with that amend. This is how I was taught to do it, and it worked for me.

One of the other tools I was taught was this. After you go through your amends and have completed them, spend some time going back through your address book, email addresses, phone or Rolodex if you use one and look for more. Because sometimes you will find people that you hadn't thought you owed amends to, and it will jog your mind and help you get them all covered for good.

Congratulations, you have completed Steps 8 and 9.

SOBER
IS JUST THE
MIDDLE GROUND
SOMEWHERE
BETWEEN MISERY
AND RECOVERY.

CHAPTER 8

DOING THE DAILY DEAL

*Whoever dwells in the shelter of the Most High
will rest in the shadow of the Almighty.*

PSALM 91:1

Now you have completed your amends, I hope you're feeling a new sense of freedom, happiness, peace and serenity. If you are, then you are ready to move on to Step 10, which is a continuation of Steps 4 and 9. You continue to make your lists and make amends. Step 10 suggests that you continue to take a daily personal inventory and when wrong you promptly admit it. In the later part of Chapter 6 of *Alcoholics Anonymous*, the authors suggest that as you do a daily inventory, you right your wrongs as you go along. They wrote that you will need to live this way of life, as you clean up the past. That you have entered what they call the "world of the spirit."

This step highlights the idea that if you continue to do a daily inventory, then when you make a mistake, you can quickly make amends and move along. It also suggests that if you are vigorously doing this in daily life, then you will have entered the world of the spirit through this process, the Spirit of God will be with you. The authors don't say, "Do this once." They don't say, "This is a one-time deal." They say that you continue your daily inventory.

GROWING IN UNDERSTANDING

The authors suggest growing in self-understanding, which takes time. It should continue all of your life. They suggest watching for selfishness, dishonesty, resentments, and fears. That when these come up, you recognize them and ask God to remove them. Just as you did in Step 7. Then discuss them with someone such as a sponsor and, if needed, immediately make amends to the individual you have harmed. You then continue to keep your thoughts on someone you can help with your experiences through love and tolerance.

The authors outline exactly how to do a daily inventory test of your action; you can correct them immediately as you go along. Not once a week or when you happen to be thinking about your mistakes. They say very specifically that you do this as you go along. Suggesting that you do this throughout each day.

They also give specific instructions to watch for selfishness, dishonesty, resentment, and fear. The authors explain exactly what to do if you spot one of these four things:

When selfishness, dishonesty, resentment, or fear crops up,
immediately ask God to remove them.

THE 10TH STEP PROMISE

Continuing with the 10th Step promise, please keep in mind that getting to this point and being able to reap the benefits of the promises means doing everything you need to do up to this point. Let's take an inventory of where you are so far.

Answer YES or NO to the following questions:

- Have I have had a 1st Step experience?
  YES/NO

- Have I found a power greater than me?
  YES/NO

- Have I made a decision to turn my life and will over to a God of my understanding?
  YES/NO

- Have I completed my inventory and shared it with another person?
  YES/NO

- Have I taken the exact nature of my wrongs to God?
  YES/NO

- Did I review where I am and become ready to ask God to remove my character defects?
  YES/NO

- Did I go to God and humbly ask Him to remove my character defects?
  YES/NO

- Have I gone through my inventory and made a list of everyone I have harmed?
  YES/NO

- Have I made direct amends to all of them that I could?
  YES/NO

- Am I making a daily inventory as I go along and promptly making amends when wrong, and am I ready to receive the promises found in Step 10?
  YES/NO

The promises found in the next part of the step are powerful. The authors suggest that because you have done the work, had the experiences, and can say YES to all of the above questions, then you can reap the benefits of the 10th Step promise:

> **We have stopped fighting anything or anyone.**
> **Our sanity has been restored.**

Ask yourself: *How would it be to go through life without fighting anything or anyone? Is this something that I would like to experience?*

The authors also say that sanity or your thinking will have been restored. You won't be interested in drugs or alcohol. Instead, you will recoil as you would from a flame. You find that you are automatically acting more normally. Without effort, you have a new attitude toward alcohol, drugs, or your problems.

The miracle is not fighting anything anymore, even addiction. And being in a safe, protected place. You haven't even sworn off drugs, alcohol, or your problems, but instead, they have been removed. You won't even have any ego about these new experiences, it is just how you'll live as long as you keep spiritually fit.

You will find that you become more interested in helping others.

You will find that these things are happing naturally and without thought. You will find yourself wanting to give more. The best part is that the more you give, the more God will give you to give more!

Having gone through all of the steps up to this point and have had the experiences and received the promises that are guaranteed if you do the work, it's time to stop and ask some questions.

Ask yourself:

- *Have I ceased fighting anything?*
- *Am I arguing with anyone?*
- *Am I interested in alcohol or drugs?*
- *Do I recoil when tempted by alcohol or drugs?*
- *Have my problems faded?*
- *Is my thinking more normal?*
- *Do I have a new attitude toward my problems?*
- *Do I feel safe and protected?*

If you are still experiencing these things at this point, then you are receiving the promises held within Step 10. You will continue to experience these things if you are in fit spiritual. This has been my personal experience. If I just take the time to check in with God every day asking for my daily set of instructions and then listen for them to come, then I don't have any fear or temptation to drink alcohol. In this manner, I keep myself spiritually fit. It's like I have a suit of steel armor on at all times. Even if there was a bottle of vodka on the table in front of me and I was alone, it wouldn't tempt me. I would recoil from it as if from a flame just like the authors say. As long as I keep myself spiritually fit and connected to God, I am invincible to alcohol. I can't drink. My God won't let it happen.

What's more, nothing can affect me physically, financially, mentally, or spiritually. "You want to rob me and steal my money, you say? That's okay, God's just going to give me more money." "You want to take away my car, my home, my possessions, you say? That's okay, God's just going to give me more cars, a new home, and more possessions." Cut me off in traffic, that's okay, you just need the road more than me."

The authors caution about being complacent about your spiritual program of action because then you aren't cured of alcoholism, drug addiction, or issues but having a daily reprieve which is contingent on the condition of your spirituality. Every day you must seek to live your life in God's will, asking how you can best serve. Asking for knowledge of his will and the power to carry it out. God's will must be done daily in order to remain free.

Okay, if you're willing to continue to make daily amends, and you can answer yes to all of the prior questions, then congratulations, you have finished Step 10.

THE
BEST PART
IS THAT
THE MORE
YOU GIVE,
THE MORE GOD
WILL GIVE YOU
TO GIVE
MORE!

CHAPTER 9

PRAYER AND MEDITATION

Prayer without mediation is like asking God
for something you don't really want.

—R. CORD BEATTY

Before moving on to the final two steps, I would like to pause and share some information on meditation that I learned in a 12 step workshop because it will become very relevant in the next three steps.

A large portion of the work in *Alcoholics Anonymous* and the 12 principles were originally taken from the Oxford Group in which the early AA groups participated. The Oxford Group was a Christian organization founded by American Christian missionary

Dr. Frank Buchman. He believed that the root of all problems was fear and selfishness. He believed the solution was to surrender our lives over to "God's plan."

Eventually, the AA members left the Oxford Group and broke off to start Alcoholics Anonymous. What I learned in this process that there are "four standards" in the Big Book:

- Selfishness
- Dishonesty
- Resentment
- Fear

The complete opposite of these are called the "four absolutes" which the early members of AA took from the Oxford Group, they are:

- Honesty
- Unselfishness
- Love
- Purity

In other words, the opposite of selfishness is unselfishness, the opposite of dishonesty is honesty, the opposite of resentment is purity, and the opposite of fear is love.

What this means to us is that guidance through prayer and meditation that appears selfish, dishonest, resentful, or fearful will clearly be from us—from our own thinking. If this is true, then wouldn't it be safe to say that guidance from prayer and meditation that is unselfish, honest, loving, and pure is clearly then from God?

When you get into Step 11, you will find that the authors say that you need to seek guidance through prayer AND meditation.

Ask yourself: *Do I consider that meditation is, in fact, listening?*

Also, please consider that there is no right or wrong way to meditate and listen.

LEARNING TO MEDITATE

A few years ago, I went all the way to Nepal to a Monastery high in the Himalayas, thinking I needed to meditate with monks for days to find some answers. Some might say that this was the wrong approach. But it worked for me. I gained a tremendous understanding of meditation from those guys. What works for one person may not work for another. Similarly, it will become very important for you to find a way that works for you.

Prayer without mediation isn't an effective way to get the answers you need. It's like asking for something you really don't want to have happened. You won't receive any direction doing this. When my sponsor explained this to me, he said that in any relationship there is talking and there is listening. There is two-way communication. If there is talking and no listening, is there really a relationship? No. You need to talk to him and then listen to the answers. Meditating and listening for the answers that you need.

If you're not practicing meditation as part of your daily prayer, then you won't receive any direction, knowledge of God's will, or the power to carry it out. If you are praying, then you are still directing the ship. You are still operating on self-will rather than living a spiritual life.

Every person I have worked with that has relapsed, has done so for one good reason. They stopped praying and meditating! This includes me. Every relapse has always come down to the issue of prayer and meditation. When I stop communicating and listening, I have no defense. I am no longer in a spiritual fit condition. Relapse is imminent!

In the early 1940s, the members of AA in the Cleveland and Akron area did what they called "Daily Written Meditation." They would write down what they were going to pray and meditate about, and then after they prayed, they would meditate. Then they would write down the guidance they received verbatim—no discussions, no editing, or input from others was acceptable. Then they would take everything that they had written down and test it against the four absolutes to see if it was honest, loving, pure, and unselfish. If it was, then they were assured that it had come from God. If it wasn't, they didn't move in that direction.

So if you take this suggestion and work through the same exercise, I believe you will have the same experiences and be able to identify the origin or where the guidance came from. Whether it came from God or if it came from them. Here is a couple of examples of this that might help. Let's assume the guidance received was, "I want to give that guy a piece of my mind." Is this honest, pure loving and unselfish? No, this came from me.

How about, "Today I need to be patient and kind to others?" Is this honest, pure loving and unselfish? Yes, this came from God.

Another example: "Don't look for faults in others. Accept them for who they are." Is this honest, pure loving and unselfish? Yes, it is.

You can go through this exercise on your own, and you will find the same results as you work through the items you wish to pray and meditate about in your daily lives.

As you move into Step 11, make this your daily routine for a week, and try it on. See how this works out for you. If it works the way it worked for all of those people in the 1940s and the way it has worked for me for several years, then make it your own daily practice. You will find this to be the essence of Step 11. All of the guidance you receive, write it down and then test it against the four absolutes. Then share what you've received from God with your sponsor or another person whom you are close to, and you will have the experience as it is meant to be.

The purpose of this is to show you that God does exist and does guide you when you pray and meditate. If you are willing to complete this exercise, you will be a great example to someone else who needs this in their lives.

If you are doubtful that this could be true, then consider how many books are available on meditation. Each one of them has something in the title that will give you a clue that it may contain information that you don't have. The word "meditation" is in the title. There is no right or wrong way to do this when you begin doing a daily exercise of prayer and meditation.

A routine that works for me is to go into the office early in the morning when it is quiet. I kneel down and pray for the daily instructions I need from God and the power needed to do his will today. When I am done, I then leave my computer turned off. Turn off my phone, and I sit at my desk with my eyes closed, and I breathe slowly, and I stay very quiet and listen.

I have also done some of my best prayers and meditation while driving. Talking to God and then listening while driving is very easy and works for me. The main thing is to not have a lot of distractions around you. You need a quiet peace and surrounding so that the prayer and meditation aren't interrupted or stopped. Let it happen by picking the right place and time to do this. You're now ready to begin Step 11.

STEP 11

Step 11 asks that you have:

> **Sought through prayer and meditation to improve your conscious contact with God as you understand Him, praying only for knowledge of His will for us and the power to carry that out.**

As I described above, to do this simply write down your prayer and meditation and then compare what you receive in meditation with the four absolutes—honesty, unselfishness, love, and purity. Asking yourself daily if the answers you receive in meditation are honest, unselfish, loving, and pure.

The authors wrote about receiving strength and direction from the one who has all power and knowledge.

Ask yourself: *If I have a source that has "all" power and knowledge, where would the best place be to go ask where to find the power and knowledge I need?*

From that source, would you agree?

So at this point, you have to start to believe that the one thing that has caused you more problems than anything else is thinking.

You have a problem and where do you take it? To your own head. Not to the one who has all power, all knowledge. If I had understood how easy this was going to be from the beginning, I would have become sober a lot sooner. If you are really self-delusional (as you read in Steps 2 and 3), then you are driven by a hundred forms of fear, self-delusion, self-seeking, and self-pity. If you are truly self-delusional, then how can you ever know if you are deluded in your thinking?

Ask yourself: *Is there any way that I can rely on myself to make it through and not drink?*

If your answer is NO, then you have knowledge and power, and by maintaining the strict disciplines of Steps 10, 11, and 12, you won't drink again no matter what!

BECOMING GOD-CONSCIOUS

The authors wrote that following God's instructions, you will begin to feel his spirit. You will become what they call "God-conscious," and it will become like a sixth sense. This is an amazing promise. And they aren't talking about alcohol but an ability to be free from your own minds. Your thinking. This sixth sense is essential for sobriety. It says you must go further and that means more action. Then it goes on to suggest prayer and meditation and not being shy about it.

I can tell you that this alcoholic doesn't want to do this. I don't want to do these disciplines every day. No, I would rather be doing what I want to do. I would rather be fly fishing, playing golf, climbing mountains, or flying airplanes to keep my sobriety. But my experience with my disease has shown me that those things don't keep me sober. Don't keep me spiritually fit.

So why am I willing to do the disciplines? Because I need to be free from alcohol. Being in a place of neutrality, safe, and protected from alcohol. That's why I do these disciplines. Not because I want to do them. It's because I enjoy the feeling of being safe and protected.

Step 11 involves prayer and meditation, and many better people use this principle, so why shouldn't we? The authors wrote that it would be easy to be vague about prayer and meditation, but it is necessary to take this valuable step.

THE EVENING REVIEW

The authors clearly describe how to do the evening review by asking yourself a series of questions before you retire at night. I have found this to be very useful in maintaining the discipline of Step 11.

The review includes asking the following questions:

- *Where have I been resentful, dishonest, selfish, and full of fear?*
- *Do I owe anyone an amends today?*
- *Have I kept anything to myself that should have been discussed with God or someone else?*
- *Have I been kind and loving toward others?*
- *What could I have done better?*
- *Have I been self-seeking today, or did I put others' needs before mine?*

On further review, don't worry or ponder negative things that happened during the day. The authors instruct that after doing your review, ask God's forgiveness and then ask God what you can do to correct anything that you are doing wrong. Meaning that after you do the review, you need to pray and meditate. You need to ask God and then listen.

As I described earlier in this chapter, if you only pray and don't meditate, then you aren't completing Step 11. You won't receive God's will and the power to carry it out. I say again, this has been one of the biggest problems in my sobriety. Praying and not meditating. I pray and don't listen, and by doing so, I create more unmanageable situations than the ones I am praying for guidance because I fail to listen.

THE MORNING REVIEW

The authors go on to instruct us on how to do your morning review. That's when you wake and ponder the day ahead. To consider your plans, have a word of prayer and ask God to direct your thinking. Asking that your thinking be void of dishonesty or self-seeking motives. Through this, you'll find you gain confidence in your actions for the day.

God gave us brains to use, so we should use them. Starting your day this way will put you on a much higher plane of thinking that is clear of unacceptable motives (thought life). The authors go on to say that they don't struggle but to let the answers come naturally.

In Steps 4 to 9, the authors talk only about your conduct—where you were wrong, self-seeking, selfish, dishonest, etc. Now the authors have moved into what they call the "thought life" of thinking. Your daily life of thinking suggests you will be on a much higher plane now that your motives are clear. You are not asking God to keep you sober just for today but asking, "Have I conceded to my innermost self that I don't have the power to keep me sober and so I have given my life and my will over to a power greater than me to keep me sober? And if I am sober now—then what is it that is keeping me sober?"

Here is something that my sponsor pointed out to me that I think is important. If I am sober and I have worked through all of the steps, then why do I need to ask God to keep me sober just for today? The compulsion to use alcohol has been removed from me. How many times do you hear someone in an AA meeting say, "I ask God to keep me sober just for today."?

Take Steve, for example, who has 23 years of sobriety and usually catches a meeting every day somewhere no matter where he is at. Before I went through the steps in this manner, the way it was done in the 1940s, it made sense to me that when he shares in meetings, he always says, "I'm Steve and I am a grateful recovering alcoholic, and I am grateful that God has kept me sober today."

To my knowledge and reading of the Big Book nowhere in there does it suggest that the key to sobriety is attending a meeting every day, talking to your sponsor every day and asking God to keep you sober just for today. If you are asking God to keep you sober one day and time, then would you agree that you may be living your life with reservation about your disease and who you are?

If you are living your life with reservation about who you are and what you need to do to not drink, then you might want to stop here and start over at Step 1 and examine if you have admitted that you are alcoholic and then do the work to see if your life is unmanageable. This is exactly what my sponsor did with me.

When we got to this point in the step work, he turned to me and asked me what I thought I needed to do to stay sober. I immediately told him that I needed to attend meetings, read the book, work with him as my sponsor, and pray every day for God to keep me sober. He shut the book and said, "So we begin. We start over!" And we did.

If you are living with some reservations at this point, then you must believe that you are in control of your drinking, and your problems are still manageable. What the authors are doing is giving us a plan of action to direct our thinking. They aren't saying that all we have to do is ask God every day to keep us sober.

The authors wrote that if you plan not to drink, you must not have any reservation or lurking notion that you can drink again someday and be immune to alcohol.

Ask yourself: *Do I have any reservations at this point about the possibility that I might be able to use drugs or drink again and be able to manage it?*

The authors also talk about the "real alcoholic." The guy who goes out on a binge and then his family members ask him if he wants to quit for good and if he is willing to go to any extreme to do so.

My experience in going in and out of AA, and in and out of one treatment center after another, never finding a way to quit drinking like so many others do, was that I wasn't willing to go to God and ask him to remove the compulsion to drink from me for good! I was living with a reservation that maybe, just maybe, I really didn't want him to do this for me. Maybe I wanted to leave a little crack in the door, just in case, I wanted to sneak out and have a drink.

Asking God to remove this from me for good means, I am willing to go to any spiritual length to keep sober because I don't have the power to do it on my own. This means that I need to call on power from a God of my understanding. This means that I have to fully commit to this with no reservation or lurking notion!

My sponsor's point was that if I was having resistance to anything that I was hearing, it was only because I hadn't experienced it for myself. I hadn't done the work and had the experience. When I first heard this, it made perfect sense. So I kept an open mind while we went through the steps again, and I became sober. The compulsion to drink was removed from me, and I had my own experience with this for the first time. I experienced the power of God!

The point is this. The reason I had an internal conflict and continued to ask God every day to keep me sober just for today was that I hadn't yet had an experience of God's power. I hadn't yet really done the work needed in all 12 Steps. As I've said before, I am a real alcoholic. The real deal. I need to get through these steps as quickly as possible. I am the guy that the authors talk about. There is no sufficient reason given that is going to keep me sober. I need power—God's power—and I need to get to it right now. Not six months from now. Right now!

In taking me through these steps, my sponsor pointed out to me that in all of the years that he had been taking people through the steps, he had never found anyone that he thought should go through the steps slowly. He said that you can't go through the steps too quickly, but you can surely take them through the steps to slowly. This has been my experience, as well.

This may be a direct reflection of the declining numbers and success of this program. What were these guys doing in the 1940s in the Akron and Cleveland Ohio area to have a 75–90 percent success rate? Think about this for a minute. What were they doing that we aren't doing now?

Advancement of medicine is far greater now than back then. There were no treatment centers for alcohol and drug addiction in the 1940s. They only had drying-out hospitals or sanitariums. Modern physiology is far more advanced in the clinical studies of alcoholism than back then. They had fewer resources and greater success. Why was this? The same spiritual instructions found in the first 103 pages of *Alcoholics Anonymous* exist today as they did back in the 1940s. So what is so different now? Interpretation of the Big Book and the 12 Steps over the years had made the process much different from when they taught it in those days. Consider this for a minute.

Could the interpretation of the process of the 12 Steps have changed so much from how it was taught in the 1940s that it has affected its success rate? Could it be that the decline in success is due to our sponsor's interpretations of the process?

Telling a newcomer that he can't sponsor someone else until he has gone through the steps and had months and months of sobriety? Could it be that telling a newcomer that it will take 6–12 months to complete the steps is flawed? Could it be that we have sponsors telling newcomers that they can't work on their 4th Step for at least six months? Have you ever heard this one? You can't sit as secretary or chair of a meeting without 12 months of sobriety under your belt? Where in the Big Book are these suggestions written?

We agree to practice the principles of the 12 Steps in all our affairs if we are to be sober. So again, might we consider that if it's not in the Big Book, it isn't the 12 Steps? If we are agreeing to practice these principles as they were written, then why are we changing what worked for hundreds of thousands of men and women before us? Something to think about.

What I do know is this. The way that the 12 Steps was taught in the 1940s had power! As we discussed before, they took newcomers through the steps, typically in 2–3 days, and then introduced them to the AA fellowship, not the other way around.

The fact that they cared more about getting someone through the steps quickly and then to meetings instead of quickly to meetings and slowly through the steps may have something to do with it.

DAILY PRACTICE AND THE 11TH STEP PROMISE

Before going through the promises of prayer and meditation here follows a recap of the instructions to keep in mind:

You don't need to ask God to keep you sober— he is already doing that.

When you wake to ponder the day ahead, consider your plans for the day and have a word of prayer and ask God to direct your thinking, so it's divorced from self-pity, dishonest, or self-seeking motives. Then say another prayer, asking for inspiration to be able to do God's will today and the power to carry it out. I also ask God to help me to remain peaceful, collected, and relaxed thought my day. Never do I ask God to keep me sober today. He already is doing that.

Then turn to meditation, listen, and quietly ask: "What would you have me do today to do your will? Who would you have me help today? Then listen further." Most of the time, my daily meditation and inspirations that I receive are simple. I am inspired to take it easy today. To be kind, generous, loving, and fearless. The point is to listen . . .

I can guarantee if you practice this as part of your daily routine, your life will change very quickly. But keep in mind that your recovery isn't only contingent on prayer and meditation. It is contingent on a daily reprieve in our spiritual condition. You need to practice all of the principles every day, not just prayer and meditation. But these two are very important, and they have been very instrumental in my own experience and life.

Okay, let's look again at the promises of Step 11. What used to be just a hunch to us, gradually is becoming a working part of your mind. You are inexperienced and have just made conscious contact with God, you aren't going to be guided clearly at all times. You will find that your thinking will become clearer and more of an inspiration that you can rely on to more you continue to pray.

Notice they use the word "gradually," meaning it takes some time. Then they go on to say, don't expect to be inspired at all times or discouraged if it is not given at all times. Remember what you read at the beginning of the 11 Step: it works if you have the right attitude and work at it.

Isn't this a beautiful promise? It tells us to be patient, and it will come. It tells us that our lives are going to change if we do. So we finish our prayer and meditation, and then we need to take more action. Meaning that we need to pray after meditation as well. We're also told that we'll make mistakes as we go along, which is why we need to follow these instructions.

First, you are going to pray and meditate in the morning: pray, meditate, and then pray again to thank God for the answers given. Then do Step 10 during the day as you go along, and then at night, do a daily review and then prayer and meditation to finish.

Through this process, there should only be one result. I can tell you from my experience that following this process, there has been only one result for me. I am either getting better, more connected spiritually or I am getting worse because I am not practicing every day.

The more you practice these principles. The more you are around others that also follow, the more you will start to notice those that do and those that don't. Those that do are happier. They are relaxed more than others. They don't take themselves too seriously.

So now you're at the end of Step 11—and accustomed to the practice of using written meditation exercises, writing down the guidance you receive and testing it against the four absolutes—I would like you to share this experience with someone else, such as a sponsor, friend, or family member.

Congratulations on completing Step 11.

RECOVERY
ISN'T ONLY
CONTINGENT
ON PRAYER AND
MEDITATION.
IT IS CONTINGENT
ON A DAILY
REPRIEVE IN OUR
SPIRITUAL
CONDITION.

CHAPTER 10

HERE AT LAST

No matter how hard your struggles are in this life, remember this; You will always be a son or daughter of a King!

—R. CORD BEATTY

Remember what we talked about in the beginning? The real work begins at Step 12. The first 11 steps are critical to getting us to a place of spiritual awakening, but Step 12 is the cement that holds it all together. It is the key to our long-term sobriety. It will keep us spiritually fit for the rest of our lives. Step 12 in *Alcoholics Anonymous* tells us: "Having had a spiritual awakening as a result of these steps, we tried to carry this message to alcoholics, and to practice these principles in all our affairs."

First, let's start by breaking down this step into three parts:

1. "Having had a spiritual awakening as a result of these steps."

2. "We tried to carry this message to alcoholics who still suffer."
3. "We practice these principles in all our affairs."

Up to this point, the steps have been preparing you to be able to do the real work in sobriety. Preparing you to help others who still suffer—and this will greatly help you with your own sobriety.

When you finished reading the Big Book, you may have noticed that Chapter 7 is entirely devoted to working with others who still suffer. The authors give specific instructions for what to do next—a road map. You have completed all of the steps to this point. You've had a spiritual awakening. You've experienced a physic change. You've finished your inventory, made your amends, swept your side of the street clean, made a decision, and then turned your life over to the care of God as you understand Him. You are now ready to go out in the world happy, sober, and spiritually fit and so able to help others who still suffer. So how do you do this? This chapter tells you exactly how to do it. What to say, what not to say, when to say it, when not to say it, what to do and what not to do.

The Big Book tells you that working with others who suffer will ensure your immunity from alcohol and because:

"You can help when no one else can. You can secure their confidence when others fail. Remember, they are very ill."

Ask yourself: *Is it essential to my sobriety and immunity from my addiction to work with others who still suffer?*

FINDING NEW MEANING

The authors suggest that life will take on a new meaning if you do so. That you must not miss the experience of watching someone be successful from going through the 12 Steps. You don't want to miss out on watching the loneliness fade away and seeing them recover.

They suggest keeping close contact with newcomers because helping them, keeps us sober.

I can tell you with conviction that nothing in my sobriety has ever given me more joy, freedom from my addiction, and personal gratification than watching someone I am sponsoring recover. The glimmer of hope in their eyes. The happiness they feel. The excitement of sobriety and seeing their spiritual awakening is something that I would hope you would want to experience. It has kept me sober and in the right place spiritually and mentally for many, many years, and will continue to do so for many more to come. Next, let's go over some instructions on how you can start to help others with our experiences.

When finding a new prospect, start by asking everything about him or her. If this individual doesn't want to quit, don't waste time on them. You might ruin the opportunity to work with them when they are ready. Talk to their family and tell them to be patient and help them realize that they are dealing with a very sick person. If they want to stop using or find solutions to life problems, then talk to the person who is most interested in them, such as their partner or spouse. Get some background on their behavior, problems, and seriousness of their condition. Find out what you can about their religious beliefs. The point is you need the information to see how to be approach and help this individual.

See the person one on one and, if possible, engage in general conversation. Tell them about your own experiences, and encourage them to talk about themselves. If they are willing to talk, then let them. You might get a better idea of how to proceed with them. In the initial conversations, you shouldn't say anything about how this is all going to be accomplished. Be careful not to lecture, talk down to, or demoralize them.

As a suggestion, describe yourself as an alcoholic, addict, or someone with other issues—whatever the case may be. Tell the person how you used to be baffled just like they are. Tell them of your struggles that led to your decision to stop. When you complete your interview and are convinced, they are the real alcoholic or addict, then talk about the hopelessness of the disease. Talk about the compulsion to drink, the phenomenon of craving once you have the first drink. Be careful not to brand this person as an alcoholic, addict, or talk about the Big Book unless they have seen it first.

If your new prospect decides to stay with the idea that they can still control their drinking and disease, tell them that they possibly can if they aren't alcoholic. But do explain this is a progressive disease that doesn't discriminate and focus mostly on your personal experiences with the disease.

When working with others, continuously reinforce your own experiences with the man or woman you are talking to. The reason for this is because you've had the experience of the 12 Steps. They haven't. They don't have a reference point to help them understand the very issues they are dealing with in their addiction. All you are doing at this point is sharing your stores of experiences with alcoholism and your experiences with sobriety.

Next, you should tell the person what happened to you. Be emphatic if the person doesn't agree with your conception of God. Tell them they can choose any conception of God or higher power they like, providing it makes sense to them. The main point is they are willing to believe in something greater than themselves. Everyone has their own interpretation of God or a higher power. It is their own choice and not one you should try to change based on your own beliefs. If the individual isn't interested or is just there to ask for favors or money, you should drop them until they agree to accept help.

Be mindful not to be discouraged if your prospect doesn't respond at once. Move on and try with someone else. You will find someone desperate enough to accept what you have to offer. It is a waste of time to keep chasing someone who isn't ready to listen. Leave them alone until they have suffered enough. Spending too much time may take away the opportunity you could have given to someone else who is ready to listen.

IT'S NOT ABOUT THEM

When I first started sponsoring others, I found out something important that I wasn't expecting. Most of the guys I was sponsoring didn't stay sober. They went back out in surprisingly short periods. I found it discouraging, to say the least. Then I read about how the first 12 guys that Bill Wilson sponsored didn't stay sober. He complained to his wife about this, and her reaction was profound. She said, "You are." That made a lot of sense to me. It doesn't matter if they stay sober or not. My job is not to keep them sober. My job is to take this message to them in the "hope" that it might help them.

Nowhere in the Big Book does it say to wait for the newcomer to come to us. Can you imagine where we would be today if Bill Wilson and Dr. Bob kicked back and said newcomers needed to come to them?

Our responsibility in living Step 12 is to seek out newcomers.

When I attend meetings, and they ask, "Is there anyone here willing to be a sponsor?" I raise my hand, and I say, "Hi, my name is Cord, and I am a grateful recovered alcoholic. If there is anyone here who needs a sponsor, see me after the meeting, and I will help you."

You see, I have a responsibility. I am simply sharing with the newcomer what my sponsor taught me to do. I am not going to wait for them to come to me. I am going to make myself available to them. I carry a blank white business card with me to each meeting I attend. On the card is my phone number and the words; "R. Cord Beatty, Alcoholic-Addict At Large!"

So when I am at a meeting, and a newcomer stands up and lets everyone know who they are and that they are new, I approach them after the meeting. I don't ask if they want a sponsor. I tell them that I am available to be a sponsor and to help them through the steps. If they say, I am looking for or needing a sponsor, I say, "You are looking at him." I let them know they have one now should they choose to let me help them. It's about taking responsibility for taking this message to other alcoholics. You see, I can't be free from my own addiction by not working with others who need help. I don't care or put energy on others and what they do. I simply do the work that I am responsible for doing, sponsor others, and help them through the steps.

This is what we are supposed to do. Going to meetings every day, reading the Big Book, socializing with the fellowship of AA isn't enough for me. I must work with others and help them, or I won't stay sober. This has been my experience.

Ask yourself: *What would happen to the 12 Steps today if everyone did exactly as I'm doing in this process? In the same way that I have been through the steps so far? Would the numbers of success in AA be less than 5 to 10 percent today? Or would it be 90 to 95 percent of all newcomers finding sobriety and staying sober as it was in the 1940s?*

We have a responsibility when we go to meetings to carry the message of hope to the alcoholic who still suffers. This doesn't mean telling everyone else my problems. This isn't sponsorship. It's what talking over a cup of coffee or a one on one meeting is meant for.

Here is an example of this. You go to meetings, and you dump all your crap on everyone else. You stand up, and you tell everyone how miserable your life is. How hard it is for you to be who you are. How your sober life just sucks beyond compare? You whine and complain and go on making the meeting all about you and your load of crap, and there is a newcomer in the meeting listening to this. It's their first meeting of AA, and this is what they experience, so they leave and never come back. We probably just lost someone we could have helped.

The point I am making is this. Those of us who have gone through the steps and have had a spiritual awakening and are sober have a responsibility to take a message of hope to the meetings. So when a newcomer arrives, and he hears a message of hope, they will want to come back. They will say, "Hey, that wasn't so bad? I heard a message of hope that I haven't heard before. I am definitely going back to another one of those meetings."

KIND ACTS

Okay, let's move on. The authors tell us that the foundation of recovery is through helping others. However, a kind act once in a while is not enough. Do this daily. It may mean interrupting your life to help someone else. Sharing your home, counseling upset wives, or husbands, going to court, hospitals, and jails just to help someone who is suffering.

As you can see, you may need to make sacrifices to help others. You may need to go to places that make you uncomfortable. Spending time and money to help others, no matter what it takes.

So when you meet a fellow alcoholic who needs your help, it's important to let them know that their recovery isn't dependent on other people but on a relationship with God or higher power. Tell them that you have seen families walk away and never return, and seen families come back.

This is where meditation and prayer will help you develop a relationship with God because you have to spend time with him. Consider this, if you are going to develop a relationship with anyone you have to spend time with them, am I correct? You have to listen. You have to communicate, or the relationship won't work. A relationship doesn't involve you doing all the talking¬—it involves talking and listening.

Both you and the new prospect must work together on spiritual progress. We know that placing these things in God's hands has an outcome far better than anything we could have planned. Following the directions of a higher power will free you from addiction. If you put your life in God's hands and have faith in his abilities, remarkable things will happen. Better than anything you could have ever imagined.

Step 12 tells us to be of maximum usefulness to others. Never hesitate to be helpful. Never hesitate to go anywhere to assist someone who is suffering. God will protect you while you do his work. The authors are defining your responsibility. Your responsibility is to take to deliver a message of hope. Take them through the steps and show them love and support. Stay on course, and your reward is sobriety and happiness. Doing this work is like wearing an impenetrable coat of armor. As long as you are doing this work, you can't fail in sobriety. You will be protected, and you will be safe.

My experience has been that this is true. In my many years of sobriety, the only thing that has ever caused me harm was complacency. The only thing that has ever taken me backward towards a relapse has been a lack of communication with God, and by not doing the work that I promised him I would do. I can also tell you with the conviction that as long as I am doing the work. Sharing the message of hope with others and working with them on the 12 Steps, I am unstoppable in my sobriety.

Your responsibility is to work with them through the steps. It isn't to do the work for them and help them fake it. Your job is not to call them every day and hound them about doing their work on the 4th Step. Asking them if they meditated or prayed today isn't your job. You have to let them experience this for themselves.

HOW WILLING ARE YOU TO BE FREE?

When I was working through the steps this way with my sponsor and was at this point in my process, he sat me down and talked to me. He asked me a few questions and asked, "How free do you want to be?" Then he asked, "Are you willing to do anything to be sober?" And I said yes. He asked, "Are you willing to go to any length to have a spiritual experience?" And I said yes. He asked, "Would you consider my experience, knowledge, of the 12 Steps and spirituality greater than yours?" And I said yes. He asked, "Are you willing to do everything that had been suggested to have what I have?" And I said yes. I wanted what he had!

However, I also said, "I've been coming in and out of meetings and sobriety for a long time." This was ultimately the problem. I had been around for a long time. I kept relapsing. Coming in and out for no reason, but my own. You could always spot me in the meetings. You could tell that I was the relapse guy running on my own self will because I would say things like, "I've put together four months of sobriety." That was the problem. I put it together. I did it all by myself, with no help from anyone. Not the 12 Steps, God, or spiritual experience. Just me on my own.

This was when my sponsor said, "Cord, you don't have anything we want. You have nothing to say that we want to hear. You have never had a spiritual awakening or experience, and you have nothing to offer. Here is a suggestion for you. Next time you go to a meeting, shut the hell up, and listen. Don't share anything, just shut up and listen. Until you've gone through the 12 Steps, fully understand the process, and had a spiritual experience, just shut up! And by the way, Cord, all that drinking you did. All the DUIs, court dates, wrecked cars, arrests, and jail time you have. The daily bottles of vodka you drank for all those years . . . Yeah . . . If we need any advice from you on how to handle that stuff, we'll call you, okay? Until then, just go to meetings, shut up, and listen!"

It was hard to hear, but so I did. Hard because I had a lot of ideas, and I wanted to share them. In all my years of going to meetings, I never had a spiritual experience. I always shared in meetings, but I was sharing someone else's experience. Experiences that I had really never had. I was there in the meetings sharing something just to be sharing something, meaning nothing. Just like everyone else that does this, I was lying to myself and everyone around me.

People would be talking about making amends or turning their lives over to their God or a higher power, and I would say, "I know everything there is to know about making amends and higher power. Yeah, I can tell you all about that. The truth was, I had never experienced it because I hadn't done the steps.

I had read about them, listened to other stories, and therefore thought I knew what I was talking about. But I had never done them with a sponsor in this way. I had never had a spiritual experience. I never had a true experience with making amends. I never had a 4th Step experience. Never turned my life over to God's will. And herein lies the difference.

If you need a spiritual experience in your life. If you need a personal experience with the 4th Step and with making amends. If you need experience with turning your life and your will over to God as you understand him, don't you think it might be a good idea to talk to someone who has? To start by seeking out that person and asking them to help you?

SHARING THE MESSAGE OF HOPE

What my sponsor did was worked me through the steps very quickly because he understood just how sick I was. He understood that I needed the promises found within the 12 Steps, and I needed them right now. He worked with me through the steps over a few days and then turned me loose and said, "Now go forth young man and share this message of hope with someone else." I was horrified. I thought for sure that I was going to kill someone.

The truth is this. I wasn't going to hurt anyone. No one was going to die from my sharing of the message of hope. People around me gave me a lot of crap over it too. They would say, "You haven't been sober long enough to sponsor someone. You haven't been sober long enough to work with someone through all 12 Steps."

Is there anywhere in the Big Book that says that you have to be sober for over a year before you sponsor someone else? No! Is there anywhere in the Big Book that it says that you have to have any length of sobriety before you can help someone though these Steps? No! So why then is it that people in AA tell us this? In my opinion, it's because of the personal interpretation of Step 12. Or maybe because they have never completed the steps themselves?

Bill Wilson wasn't sober for a year before he sponsored his first person. Dr. Bob wasn't sober a year before he carried this message to someone else. They were only sober a few days! The book says that the only prerequisite is that I have completed all 12 Steps and that I have had a spiritual awakening, and now I have something to offer. So I should sponsor someone else and help them through the steps.

My experience with this is that there have been very few things in my life that have given me more joy than helping someone else who suffers from addiction. There isn't a real way to explain the feeling of this joy until you have experienced it for yourself. Only someone who has done this can truly understand this.

When talking with someone who still suffers, never show any hatred toward alcoholism or addiction. This won't help when talking to someone who is still suffering. If you show intolerance toward addiction, your prospect might walk away when you could have helped them. Someone who is still drinking will be intolerant of anyone that says they hate drinking.

It has not always been that way over the years. I have sponsored guys who I didn't want to work with at first. I have sponsored a few people in the past that harbored so much anger, resentment, and negativity that they could suck the very oxygen out of a room simply by walking into it. They would call me up and whine about everything and everyone. Whine about their wives, kids, job, and hated everyone and everything. When they called, I would cringe and say oh hell . . . "Dudley Downer is on the line again. Here we go . . . I've got to listen to this bankrupt broken crap for another hour. I'd rather be high jumping into a pool filled with broken shards of glass than to listen to this pathetic ass again. Now I've got to call my sponsor and whine about the complaining this guy just did with me."

But even in these times, I can tell you something that may

surprise you. Inevitably without fail, somewhere in the course of the discussions of the 12 Steps with these individuals, something magical happened, and my attitude toward them would change. I would begin to have gratitude toward these individuals and for my own sobriety.

I would always go home, and during my daily prayer, say, "Thank you, God, for allowing me to do this with this man. Thank you for placing him in my life where I could be a tool to do your work because this man really needs this message from you. Thank you for allowing me to teach him and him to teach me."

This is one of the greatest things about the 12 Steps and the fellowship of AA. We are all in this together. The newcomer needs us because they have been around for a while and can offer sponsorship, and the old-timers need the newcomers. It's a fascinating process to be involved with.

I want to welcome all of you who have taken this journey with me. When we set out, I asked you a few questions about what you believe about addiction, alcoholism, your own experiences, and beliefs.

QUESTIONS ON BELIEFS

In closing, I would like to go over a few things with you again. If you remember, these came from a handout titled "Questions on Beliefs in AA." As we go through them, I will offer an explanation in hopes that they are clearer to you now and that you have a better understanding of them.

1. *If I am planning to stop drinking, all I have to do is not drink one day at a time?*
FALSE: The authors wrote, If you're planning to stop

drinking, there must be no reservations that you might be immune to alcohol.

2. Once I complete the steps, I will have a partnership with my higher power?
FALSE: Remember the meaning of partnership? That you are willing to let God be the Director now?" Does this sound like a partnership? That you are going to have a new employer. Does this sound like a partnership? If God has all power, then is it a partnership with him? No.

3. Once I understand God, I will be free from my addiction?
FALSE: Can you really fully understand God? The only way to fully understand God is to be God. Can I really understand him? No.

4. My purpose in sobriety is to get back into the mainstream of life?
FALSE: The authors wrote that the main purpose is to be of maximum service to God and to others.

5. There are many different ways I can work on this program?
FALSE: The authors wrote that they had never seen anyone fail who had followed their path through the 12 Steps.

6. My sobriety is my greatest possession?
FALSE: Your past is your greatest asset. Frequently almost the only one. So the greatest possession, according to the Big Book, is your past.

7. It takes a long time to recover from alcoholism?
FALSE: The authors wrote that reading their book and working with another alcoholic accomplishes in a few weeks what you may have been suffering and struggling with for years. Later in the book, the authors describe how a lawyer who had only been working on the steps for three days,

completed Step 3—turned his life and will over to God—and his wife said that she saw something different in him already.

8. *The steps aren't required; they are suggested?*
FALSE: The authors wrote that none of them liked confessing their defects of character, swallowing their pride, nor the self-searching, but the process is required to be successful. It says that the steps are required, not suggested.

9. *Going to meetings and not drinking is vital to my Recovery?*
FALSE: The authors wrote that strenuous work with one another is the key to recovery.

10. *Our common suffering is what holds us together?*
TRUE: The authors wrote that sharing our common suffering brings us together. It says that because every one of us has a common solution, we are joined in fellowship together. Our suffering is not what holds us together. Our suffering brings us together. What holds us together is the common solution found in the 12 Steps.

Every single one of you who have gone through the steps with a sponsor is now in a position to mentor someone else. You are ready to share this message with another person who still suffers.

I am here to tell each and every one of you that if you have completed the Steps, had a spiritual awakening, and gone through this process, you are ready. You are the ones to take this message. We depend on you to continue to take this message to newcomers.

You have a responsibility to take this message to others. Your responsibility is to sponsor someone else and help them through the steps. You can't do this wrong. There is no school to teach you how to be a sponsor. You learn how to be a sponsor by being one. What would have happened when Bill Wilson carried the message to Dr. Bob, Dr. Bob would have said, "How long have you been sober?"

When I finished the steps in the way we have gone through them, I realized in my spiritual awakening that God had made a deal with me. He said, "Cord. I guarantee you that you will never have to drink or use again. You will never have to live the way you have been living, and all I ask is that you take this message to another person still suffering. Are you in?"

I said, "Yes, 100 percent I'm in!"

I want to ask you all the same questions that I was asked.

Ask yourself: *How free do I want to be?*

Because if you truly want to be free, free from addictions, you will take this message of hope to another who suffers. You will do the work and sponsor others.

A FINAL TASK

There is one last task I want to ask of you if you feel you are ready. It is a task that my sponsor challenged me with and one that I took head-on because I was ready. He asked me if I believe that God has all power and that he can and will do anything for me if I ask and trust in him? I said yes, I believe this with all my heart. He then challenged me to ask God to remove the compulsion to use drugs and alcohol from me for good. He added that this should be something that I only do one time in my life if I truly do have faith and use the words "for good!"

On October 10, 2010, I found myself completely ready to have God remove the compulsion to use drugs and alcohol from me for good. I was ready for God to take all of my depression, anxiety, mental health issues, and self-imposed crisis from me. I was ready to surrender all of it to him. I knelt down that day and humbly asked Him to remove all of it from me for good.

I have been free from my addictions and mental health issues from that day forward. The compulsion to use alcohol and drugs has been taken from me. My thinking has changed. I have changed. It hasn't always been easy. There have been days when I have struggled, but I am free!

Staying clean, sober and happy is a simple process. Communication with God or higher power is the cure for addictions and mental health issues. As I have said before, spirituality is the true path to recovery. Building a solid relationship with God doesn't involve you doing all the talking. It involves talking and listening.

I want to challenge you, my friends, to the same task if you feel that you are ready. Do you have absolute faith in God or a higher power at this point? Do you believe that God has all power and the ability to remove everything from you for good? Do you believe he is everything? If the answer is yes, then you should have no reservation about taking this final last step. That you ask God to remove the compulsion to use drugs and alcohol from you. And that he remove your difficulties from you for good. I ask that you do it now! This is my challenge to you.

BUILDING
A SOLID
RELATIONSHIP
WITH GOD
DOESN'T INVOLVE
YOU DOING ALL
THE TALKING.
IT INVOLVES
TALKING AND
LISTENING.

How free do you want to be?

FINAL WORDS . . .

I've now been sober for many years, and people ask me why I continue to work with addicts and alcoholics. If you're asking the same question or why I would write about this process, it's not for money but because I want to share a message of hope. It's my way of staying spiritually fit and sober. For the past several years, I've run a treatment center for alcohol and drug addiction that has never turned a profit. I've put thousands of dollars of my own money and time into that business and continue to do more every day when needed. I've helped individuals who can't afford treatment more times than I can count. I've given everything I have and 100 percent of my time, effort, and love to those suffering from addiction and alcoholism.

People ask me why? Why do you do that, Cord? Why do you throw good money after bad and spend all your time at that place?"

My answer is simple. "To give back what was so freely given to me. To give to someone else what I couldn't give myself without help from God and another person just like me."

I do it to see the light of God in another person who suffers. To watch the miracle of it all when they have their first spiritual experience. When they find sobriety for the first time. To see them reunite with family, wives, husbands, children, and friends who love and care for them. To share their happiness. I tell them the joy this brings to me is far more reward than any amount of money will ever offer me.

I love working through the steps with someone who needs the promises found in them. I can always tell the newcomers who have completed the steps. They are the happy ones who come to meetings. The one with new teeth, a new job, new clothes, new apartment, new shoes, a new haircut, and a new relationship!

I also want to bear my testimony and share my beliefs with you. I want to tell you that because of these 12 Steps and the promises found within them, I was cured of my alcoholism and addictions. I want to tell you with conviction, God lives! God is everything and everywhere around you. God hears every prayer, answers every prayer, and communicates to us in unimaginable ways. Jesus Christ is the Son of God and my savior. He suffered on the cross for every one of my sins and yours too. I have found my purpose on this earth. A purpose ordained by God and given directly to me. To help those who still suffer.

Should our paths cross again, and you need a helping hand from me, I pray that I can be of service to you. Thank you from the bottom of my heart for picking up this book and reading it. I hope that it has been an insightful and learning experience for you.

God bless.

R. Cord Beatty

ABOUT THE AUTHOR

Cord Beatty's story is one of spiritual awakening and redemption and a journey to full recovery from alcoholism and addiction. Early in adult life, he accomplished a successful career in film and television—financing and producing numerous productions and films. Along with success came the stresses of running a publicly traded corporation, raising money, managing employees, successes, and failures.

By age 46, alcohol had taken everything from Cord, including his marriage, children, business, home, automobiles, and money. Alcohol had also taken its toll on his health, and he found himself homeless and facing serious health issues. In 2010, Cord was told by doctors that he wouldn't live the day due to liver failure. Broken, bankrupt, defeated, and standing on death's door, Cord experienced the miracle of spiritual awakening and the power of God for the first time in his life.

Cord recovered from alcoholism and addiction and went back to college at Purdue University, pursuing his master's degree in Psychology in Addiction. He is now a grateful member of Alcoholics Anonymous and an active worker in the recovery community: the co-founder of New U Recovery residential inpatient treatment center near Park City Utah and the founder of The Retreat At Zion residential inpatient treatment center in Rockville Utah.

A public speaker and regular on talk shows, radio broadcasts, podcasts and was featured on the cover and feature article of *Recovery Today* magazine in 2018. Cord has helped hundreds of individuals to overcome addiction through his treatment centers, education, and sponsorship in the AA and NA programs. Cord is a father of five children and four grandchildren.

CPSIA information can be obtained
at www.ICGtesting.com
Printed in the USA
BVHW052315230322
632316BV00006B/71